FASTING FOOD

Katie Mantzarides

FASTING FOOD

LENTEN RECIPES FROM A GREEK KITCHEN

translated and arranged
by
Anna Veniamin

MOUNT THABOR PUBLISHING
2018

FASTING FOOD:
LENTEN RECIPES FROM A GREEK KITCHEN
Copyright © 2018 by Katie Mantzarides

Published by
Mount Thabor Publishing
106 Hilltop Road,
Waverly Township, PA 18414 USA

www.mountthabor.com

Printed in the United States of America

ISBN 978-0-9774983-3-8

Translated from the Seventh Greek Edition, 1994
Νηστήσημα Φαγητὰ καὶ Γλυκά (Fastworthy Foods and Desserts)
Published by P. S. Pournaras Publications
Kastritsiou 12, 546 26 Thessalonica
Greece
ISBN (Greek edition) 960-242-090-1

Front cover:
Original Oil Painting, *Church on Santorini*
Copyright © 2018 by Maria Veniamin
Printed by permission

TABLE OF CONTENTS

THE FASTS OF OUR CHURCH

THE ORTHODOX CHURCH has days and periods of fasting. The days of fasting are Wednesdays and Fridays. In addition there are the days of the Elevation of the Precious Cross (September 14), and the Beheading of Saint John the Baptist (August 29).

The periods of fasting are:

1) Great Lent, from Clean Monday up to and including Holy Saturday. However, fish is eaten on the Feast of the Annunciation (March 25), and also on Palm Sunday.

2) The Christmas Fast (November 15 to December 24), during which fish is eaten from November 21 until December 17,* excluding Wednesdays and Fridays.

3) The Dormition Fast (August 1 to August 14). On the day of the Transfiguration (August 6), fish is eaten.

4) The Fast of the Holy Apostles, which begins on the day after the Sunday of All Saints until June 28, during which fish is eaten, except for Wednesdays and Fridays.

The following exceptions apply to the aforementioned:

1) There is no fasting whatever during the period from Christmas to Theophany (except for January 5, which is a fast day), and during the three weeks which begin, respectively, with the Sunday of the Publican and Pharisee, and of Pascha (Easter), and Pentecost.

2) Cheesefare Week, during which there is fasting only from meat.

3) Fish is allowed on Wednesdays and Fridays in the following cases:

September 8 (The Birth of the Theotokos)
November 14 (Eve of Christmas Fast)
November 21 (Entry of the Theotokos)
January 7 (Synaxis of Saint John the Baptist)
February 2 (Feast of the Meeting)
June 24 (Birth of Saint John the Baptist)
June 29 (Apostles Peter and Paul)
August 15 (Dormition of the Theotokos)

4) Fish is also allowed on the Wednesday of mid-Pentecost and on the Wednesday of the Leave-taking of Pascha.

Monks and many Orthodox Christians do not eat oil when fasting on Wednesdays and Fridays, and during the fasting periods of Great Lent and the Dormition. For them the following exceptions apply: Oil is allowed on Saturdays (except for Holy Saturday), Sundays and on certain feast days mentioned in the Great Book of Hours (*Mega Horologion*).

On certain days of fasting all Christians abstain from eating oil, when they do not fall on a Saturday or Sunday: September 14, December 24, January 5, August 29.

This also applies to Clean Monday and the whole of Great and Holy Week, or at least to Holy Friday and Holy Saturday.

* See the note for November 15 in the Calendar of the Church of Greece (1986), p. 170. Some follow the practice that prevails at monasteries, according to which fish is eaten on Saturdays and Sundays only, from November 21 to December 12.

KITCHEN BASICS

OLIVE OIL

THE OLIVE OIL referred to in these recipes is always extra-virgin olive oil (EVOO). Extra-virgin olive oil is extracted from the olive fruit mechanically, cold-pressed, without heat or chemicals. It has the least acidity, the most nutrients and the best flavor. Often called 'liquid gold', extra-virgin olive oil is a food with many health benefits, and it constitutes an important part of the Mediterranean diet. It is best consumed when it is less than a year old, and should be stored away from heat and light. Once it has been opened it should be consumed within less than two months.

Although olive oil is widely available in the United States, choosing the best oil for your purpose can be as bewildering as choosing a good bottle of wine or a good cheese. Olive oils may be referred to as fruity (a characteristic often found in oils from Crete), or peppery (the oils of the Peloponnese tend to have more peppery flavors). In fact a wide variety of characteristics are to be found in the olive oils of any geographical region.

When choosing an olive oil it is important to read the label carefully. The best oils are most often the product of a particular region, with the contents of the bottle being traceable to a particular harvest. Such olive oil is however, for many of us, an investment, to be drizzled on salad greens and vegetables.

For the majority of culinary purposes, many cooks use instead a good, all-purpose blend of extra-virgin olive oil. But such a product must be purchased with great care. Since recent scandals have revealed the dishonest labeling of some of the olive oils to be found on our supermarket shelves it has become evident that we need to choose our oil wisely in order to avoid buying inferior quality vegetable oils which have been mixed and flavored to look and smell like olive oil. Good all-purpose olive oils are available, produced in Greece, in California, or elsewhere and the key to finding a satisfactory product is to research the companies involved; seeking one which is open, dependable and honest.

BREAD

BREAD is an essential component of any Greek meal. Try to buy bakery bread containing only flour, yeast, salt and water, and not wrapped in plastic. Store it in paper, or wrapped in a clean, dry cloth. Besides being a valuable accompaniment to your meal, the remains of such a loaf have important uses in the Greek kitchen.

Remove the crust from any leftovers, slice it and place it on a baking sheet. When your oven has been in use, put your tray of bread in it as you turn it off. Leave it there to toast and dry (but don't forget to take it out before you preheat your oven again.) Once it is dry, break it up and blitz it in a food processor (or place it in a zip lock bag and crush it) until you have finely ground, dry breadcrumbs. It can be stored in the freezer ready for use in your recipes.

Greek cooks also use leftover bread as a thickener in recipes such as garlic sauce. The crust is removed from the bread, which must not be fresh but slightly dry, and the bread is soaked for a minute or so in a bowl of water. It is then pressed between the palms of the hands to remove the excess water, crumbled, and added to the recipe. If you only have fresh bread available, dry it in a low oven for ten minutes or so before you soak it for use in this way. The kind of bread that comes wrapped in plastic, and contains preservatives that keep it fresh, cannot be successfully used in this way.

Herbs

Oregano

Traditionally collected from the mountains of Greece, where it is a common wild plant, oregano is dried before use and should be rubbed between the fingers as it is added to the dish. The oregano that grows in the United States is less strongly flavored then Mediterranean oregano. Since it keeps well, it is worth investing in a bag of dried Mediterranean oregano; look for it when you are buying your olive oil.

Dill

This herb is used fresh. It is easily obtainable but it doesn't store well. Don't let it spoil in your refrigerator, instead chop it finely, put it in a zip lock bag and freeze it. It will store well and be conveniently ready for use.

Parsley

The flat-leafed variety, often known as *Italian* parsley, is the best kind to use in these dishes. Both the leaves and the tender stalks of the parsley plant are used in cooking. Unlike dill, parsley does keep very well in the refrigerator. Wrap it loosely in plastic and store in on the middle shelf. If it is fresh when purchased, it will keep for 2–3 weeks in this way.

Mint

May be used fresh or dried. If it is dried, crumble it between your fingers as you add it to the dish and bear in mind that dried herbs have a stronger flavor.

Walnuts

These are often bought conveniently shelled; try to avoid those which have also been chopped, roasted or salted.

Garlic

Buy fresh garlic whenever possible. Garlic stores well in a crock at room temperature or in the crisper in your refrigerator and is easy to prepare. Crush the cloves lightly to loosen and remove the skin. If the recipe calls for garlic crushed to a paste, you can crush it, with a pinch of salt, under the flat side of your chopping knife. Alternatively, use a garlic press. These are easy to use but take a little extra time to clean; brush the press with a vegetable brush before the sticky garlic paste sets in the little holes.

TOMATOES

YOUR TOMATOES should be fresh, ripe, and locally grown, such as are available at farmers markets during summer. The Thessalonians have the benefit of Cretan imports during the cold months, but in parts of the United States good fresh tomatoes are difficult to come by in winter. In most cases, canned tomatoes make an acceptable substitute. Choose your canned tomatoes carefully; look for whole, skinned tomatoes in juice. No 'improvements' such as added herbs or garlic. Some canned tomatoes have an unpleasant metallic or acidic flavor and you may have to experiment to find a good brand.

When a recipe requires you to skin fresh tomatoes, simply dunk them, for a minute, in boiling water. After which cool them in cold water and pull off the skins. If you only need to skin one or two firm tomatoes, you can use a sharp vegetable peeler, as if you were peeling an apple or a potato. Sometimes it is necessary to seed the tomatoes for use in a recipe: Cut them in half, horizontally, and squeeze each half gently to loosen and remove the seeds.

LEMONS

THESE are an essential ingredient in many Mediterranean cuisines. Buy fresh lemons; avoid using bottled lemon juice. When the zest of the lemon is required it is wise to first ensure that the fruit is very well washed. A sprinkle of baking soda and a vegetable brush will help to remove unwanted residues from the skin. Use the fine holes of your grater on the yellow surface of the skin to obtain grated lemon zest, or a potato peeler to remove strips of zest – avoid the bitter white pith from below the yellow zest.

TAHINI

A SESAME SEED paste used to add richness and creaminess, especially in oil-free dishes. Most large supermarkets sell this, it is also found in Middle Eastern grocery stores.

EQUIPMENT

VERY LITTLE special equipment is required: A mortar and pestle is a traditional piece of equipment in most Mediterranean kitchens. Today it may be replaced by a food processor with good results. The food processor, or blender, can also do the job of the vegetable mill. There are benefits and inconveniences with both old and new systems and the choice is purely personal.

One other very convenient tool, essential to most kitchens, is a four-sided grater. This kind of freestanding grater is easier to use than most others. Some of these recipes suggest grating onion; if you prefer to avoid doing this, then use the food processor instead. Grating tomatoes is a useful way to peel and puree them in one step: Halve the tomato horizontally and rub each half, cut side against the coarse holes of your grater, until you are left holding only the skin.

A.V.

APPETIZERS

SIDE DISHES

SOUPS

SALADS

PASTAS

PIZZAS & PIES

SECTION ONE

Walnut-Garlic Sauce
Skordaliá me karydia

GARLIC SAUCE is a delicious appetizer which compliments vegetable dishes particularly well: boiled beets and fried zucchini almost demand this accompaniment. Every Greek village has a variation on this aromatic, creamy sauce, but the main point is that the garlic must be fresh and all the ingredients must be smoothly amalgamated. This is traditionally accomplished with a mortar and pestle, however a food processor makes an acceptable and efficient substitute.

> **3 slices (about 3 ounces), day-old French or Italian bread (see Note below)**
> **1/2 cup ground walnuts (about 4 ounces)**
> **3 garlic cloves, crushed to a pulp**
> **1/4 teaspoon salt**
> **1/4 cup olive oil (optional)**
> **2–4 teaspoons lemon juice or white wine vinegar**

1. Trim the bread of all crust and soak it for 1–2 minutes in a bowl of water. Press the bread between the palms of your hands to remove the excess water and crumble it into the bowl of a food processor.

2. Add the walnuts, garlic, and salt and process the mixture until well combined.

3. *To prepare the sauce with oil:* With the machine running, pour the oil in a thin stream into the walnut mixture. Add the lemon juice or vinegar and process to mix. The resulting sauce should be smooth and creamy; if it is too thick, add 1–2 tablespoons of water.

To prepare the sauce without oil: Add the lemon juice or vinegar to 1/4 cup of tepid water and, with the machine running, add to the walnut mixture in a thin stream. If necessary add a little extra water until the mixture is smooth and creamy.

Note: French or Italian bread is specified here since it begins to dry quickly. If your bread is too soft and fresh, then, having removed the crust, dry it in a low oven for a few minutes and allow it to cool before proceeding.

Preparation time: 20 minutes   Yield: 11/4 cups (serves 4)

Garlic Sauce with Eggplant and Peppers
Skordaliá me Melintsanes kai Kokkines Piperiés

EGGPLANTS are at their best in late summer. Look for smooth, glossy skins and firm, not spongy, flesh. They develop greater bitterness when they are no longer fresh - a bright green stalk indicates that they have not been lying around in the store for too long.

Roasting eggplants and peppers until they are blackened and collapsed brings a deeper, more complex flavor to this meaty, relish-like garlic sauce.

1 eggplant (about 1 pound)
2 large, sweet red peppers
1 large, sweet green pepper
2 cloves of garlic
1/2 teaspoon salt
1/2 cup olive oil
4 teaspoons vinegar
4 teaspoons Worcestershire sauce

1. Preheat the broiler (or charcoal grill).

2. Wash and dry the eggplant and peppers and prick the eggplant once or twice with a fork. Broil them, turning them from time to time, until the eggplant is dark, wrinkled and collapsed and the peppers have dark blisters on all sides.

3. When the vegetables are cool enough to handle, pull off their skins, discarding the stems and seeds, and cut them into small dice. Squeeze the eggplant dice gently between the palms of your hands and discard the juice which is expelled and which tends to be bitter. Place them, and the diced peppers, in the bowl of an electric mixer. (This can also be beaten with an egg beater or balloon whisk).

4. Crush the garlic to a purée with the salt and add it to the vegetables. Turn the mixer on at low speed and add the oil slowly.

5. Continue to beat on low speed, adding the vinegar and Worcestershire sauce according to taste.

Serve at room temperature.

Preparation time: 45 minutes   Yield: 21/2 cups garlic sauce (serves 5)

Fish Roe Spread
Taramosalata

THIS APPETIZER will turn a simple meal into a special one. It is light and creamy with a delicate pink hue.

It is made with taramas, a cured fish roe product which may be bought in jars at Greek delicatessens, or more conveniently for many of us, from one of the many importers of Greek food products to be found on the World Wide Web. You can buy taramosalata as a ready-made spread, however it is not nearly as good as the homemade version. Taramas should be stored in the refrigerator and will keep up to a week after opening.

> 3 tablespoons flour
> 1 cup water
> 4 ounces taramas (see note below)
> 2 cups olive oil
> 1/4 cup lemon juice
> 3–4 green onions, finely chopped
>   *or* 1/2 small onion, grated and drained (optional)

1. Combine the flour and the water in a small saucepan. Stir the mixture over medium-low heat until it simmers and becomes a smooth, thick batter. Remove it from the heat and allow it to cool.

2. Place the flour mixture in a food processor or, better still, in the bowl of an electric mixer. Add the fish roe and process or beat until it is combined. Continue to process or beat whilst adding the oil and lemon alternately.

3. The chopped or grated onion may added at the end. Alternatively, try adding a few drops of the juice from a grated onion.

Serve the salad in a bowl, garnished with olives.

Note: Taramas can vary significantly between brands. If yours is too salty, try rinsing it in water. This is most easily done by placing it in a sieve lined with a paper coffee filter and carefully pouring a half a cup or so of water through it. Allow it to drain well before using.

Preparation time 20 minutes   Yield 3 cups

Eggplant Dip
Melintsanosalata

THIS RECIPE relies upon the quality of the eggplant; therefore it is essential that you choose young, fresh specimens. Large and old eggplants are more likely to contain bitter juices and big, hard seeds, both of which will spoil this dish.

Serve this, with bread to dip, as an appetizer or side dish. It's smooth, airy texture contrasts nicely with many vegetable main-course dishes.

> **2 eggplants (about 1 1/4 pounds)**
> **1/3 cup olive oil**
> **1 clove of garlic, peeled and crushed to a pulp**
> **Juice of 1/2 lemon**
> **1/2 teaspoon salt**

1. Preheat the broiler.

2. Wash and dry the eggplants. Pierce the skin of the eggplants with a sharp knife in 3–4 places, this will prevent them from exploding in the oven.

3. Place them under the broiler and cook, turning occasionally, until the eggplants collapse and become dark and wrinkled on all sides. This will take about 20 minutes.

4. When they are cool enough to handle, cut them in half lengthwise and use a spoon to scoop out all the flesh. Squeeze the flesh gently between the palms of your hands, expelling and discarding the bitter juices.

5. Put the eggplant flesh in a food processor. Add the olive oil, garlic, lemon juice and salt and process until smooth and creamy. Taste and adjust the seasoning.

Preparation time: 15 minutes
Cooking time: 30 minutes

Yield: 2 1/2 cups (5 servings)

Mushroom Patties
Manitarokeftédes

LITTLE SAVORY DISHES, known in Greece as *mezedes*, are common throughout the Mediterranean. The city of Thessalonica is well-known for its many establishments serving mezedes to be enjoyed with drinks among company.

In homes they are part of the tradition of hospitality and guests in a Greek home are often served such little treats.

Whilst they do not comprise a meal in themselves they can form part of a luncheon table. They could also be served as snacks, or appetizers at dinner.

1 pound mushrooms
1 medium onion
4 tablespoons self-rising flour
3–4 tablespoons finely chopped parsley
Oil for shallow frying

1. Wash and finely chop the mushrooms (this can be done in a food processor), and place them in a mixing bowl.

2. Peel and grate the onion, or chop it very finely in a food processor.

3. Add the onion to the mushrooms, with the flour and parsley. Season the mixture with salt and pepper and mix it well. If the mixture is too wet, add a little extra flour.

4. Heat about 1/4 inch of oil in a large frying pan and add the mushroom mixture by heaped tablespoons. Fry the patties for 1–2 minutes on each side until they are golden.

Serve hot with lemon wedges to garnish.

Preparation time: 30 minutes
Cooking time: 15 minutes

Yield: 24 patties

Potato Croquettes
Patatokrokétes

A potato dough is deep fried in little portions producing light, puffed potato balls.

2 pounds potatoes
1 envelope dry yeast
1 tablespoon margarine
5 ounces (1 generous cup) all-purpose flour
1 teaspoon salt
Oil for deep frying
Tomato wedges to serve
Oregano, optional

1. Wash and peel the potatoes and boil them in salted water until they are tender. Purée them: A food mill or a potato ricer is helpful here. Alternatively simply mash them until they are smooth. Do not use a food processor or a blender since this will turn the potatoes into a glue-like paste.

2. Add the margarine and flour to the puréed potatoes and season them with the salt and some freshly ground black pepper.

3. Dissolve the yeast in a tablespoon of tepid water and add it to the potato mixture.

4. Knead the potato dough briefly and leave it, covered, in a warm place to rise for about an hour.

5. Heat 2–3 inches of oil in a deep saucepan on medium high. Reduce the heat to medium and use two teaspoons to take small walnut-sized portions of the dough and slip them into the hot oil. Do not overcrowd them; it will be necessary to fry them in batches. They will become puffed and golden within less than a minute if the oil is sufficiently hot. As soon as they are done, transfer them with a slotted spoon to a plate lined with paper towels.

Serve the croquettes hot garnished with tomato wedges. They may also be sprinkled with a little dried oregano.

Preparation time: 1 hour   Yield: about 50 small croquettes
Rising time: 1 hour

Garlic Shrimp
Garídes me Manitária

1 pound raw, frozen shrimp, peeled
3–4 cloves of garlic
5 tablespoons olive oil
1/4 cup dry white wine
2 tablespoons finely chopped parsley
Lemon wedges for serving, optional

1. Bring a large pot of water to the boil and add a little salt. Add the frozen shrimp and, after one minute, drain the shrimp. Toss them gently to remove excess water.

2. Peel and finely chop the garlic.

3. Heat the oil in a frying pan and cook the shrimp gently for 3–4 minutes. Add the garlic and the wine then simmer for 2–3 minutes until the wine is reduced.

4. Season with salt and pepper and add the finely chopped parsley.

Stir well and serve immediately with lemon wedges.

Preparation time: 20 minutes

Yield: 3–4 small servings

Fried Zucchini
Kolokythákia teganitá

ZUCCHINI is very versatile and makes an appearance in many Greek dishes. Here it is transformed into a very good appetizer.

The best zucchini are firm with glossy skins. Allow two hours for the zucchini to expel its water before cooking.

These must be served as soon as they are cooked; do not add salt until you have tasted them because they are usually salty enough after their initial salting in the colander. Walnut garlic sauce makes a very good accompaniment.

1 pound zucchini
1/2 cup flour
Oil for deep-frying

1. Peel the zucchini and cut them into thin (1/8-inch) rounds.

2. Arrange them in layers in a colander, sprinkling each layer with a little salt. Place the colander over a bowl and leave them to drain for about 2 hours.

3. Wipe the zucchini dry with paper towels. Place the flour in a bowl and toss the zucchini in the flour.

4. Fill a large saucepan to 1/3 of its capacity with oil and heat it on medium-high. When the oil is hot, take slices of zucchini and slip them carefully into the hot oil. Do not overcrowd them.

5. When the zucchini slices are golden remove them with a slotted spoon onto paper towels to drain. Continue with successive batches until all the slices are cooked.

Serve immediately.

Preparation time: 45 minutes   Yield: 4 appetizer/side servings
Standing time: 2 hours

Fried Peppers

Piperiés teganités

ITALIAN PEPPERS are the long, pale green variety of sweet pepper, which are sometimes called frying peppers. They are available year round in most supermarkets. Take care not to choose the hot peppers of similar appearance.

Make this ahead to allow time for the flavors to blend as the peppers come to room temperature. It is best eaten on the day that it made however, since it looses quality upon refrigeration.

1 pound Italian peppers
1/2 cup olive oil
2 medium, ripe tomatoes
1 tablespoon vinegar

1. Wash and dry the peppers, remove the stalks with a paring knife and carefully scoop out the seeds.

2. Heat the oil in a lidded frying pan and fry the peppers on medium-low heat, covered, until they are soft and wrinkled, this should take about 30 minutes. Protect yourself from splatters as you turn them.

3. Transfer the peppers to a serving dish, reserving the oil in the pan.

4. If the peppers have browned in places the brown papery parts of the skin may be slipped off once they are sufficiently cool.

5. Skin the tomatoes. Purée one tomato and finely chop the other.

6. Pour off all but one tablespoon of the frying oil then add the chopped and puréed tomatoes and the vinegar to the pan. Season with salt and pepper and simmer the sauce for 2–3 minutes.

7. Pour the sauce over the peppers and allow the dish to stand for one or two hours at room temperature before serving.

Preparation time: 20 minutes
Cooking time: 30 minutes
Standing time: 1–2 hours

Yield: 4 servings (as a side or appetizer)

Giant Lima Beans Baked in Tomato Sauce
Fasólia Gígantes sto Foúrno

LIMA BEANS need to be soaked before cooking. All legumes they should be sorted carefully before use: Pour them onto a clean tray, push them to one side and pass them across the tray in small batches looking carefully for foreign particles.

If they are in season, fresh tomatoes are much to be preferred in this particular dish. Grating fresh tomatoes is a very simple way to purée them and skin them whilst retaining some of their volume.

This dish is very rich and is usually eaten as an appetizer. Good bread is an essential accompaniment.

1 pound large lima beans
1 celery stalk, halved
1 carrot, peeled and halved
10–12 pepper corns
4 large onions
5 cloves of garlic, sliced
2 pounds ripe tomatoes or 2 (14-ounce) cans plum tomatoes
1 1/2 cups olive oil
Pinch of sugar
1 stick cinnamon (optional)
1/4 cup finely chopped parsley
2 tomatoes, sliced
1 tablespoon oregano

1. Sort the beans discarding any foreign particles. Rinse them well.

2. *Overnight soaking method:* Place them in a large bowl, cover them with cold water by 3–4 inches and set them aside to soak overnight (or for about eight hours).

3. *Same day soaking method:* Cover them with water and bring them to a boil, simmer them for 5–10 minutes and drain. Put them back in the pot, add sufficient fresh water to cover by about three inches and bring to the boil again. Remove them from the heat, cover and leave to soak for one hour. Continue with step 5.

4. *If you have soaked the beans overnight:* Drain and put them in a large pot, add fresh water to cover them by about two inches.

5. Add the celery, carrot and peppercorns to the pot. Simmer the beans, covered, until they are just tender (this will take between one and three hours). Drain, reserving 1 cup of the cooking liquid. Put

the beans in an ovenproof dish (a 13x9x2-inch Pyrex dish is ideal) and set it aside.

6. Peel the onions and grate them on the coarse side of a four-sided grater, or chop very finely in a food processor. Peel and slice the garlic cloves.

7. *If using fresh tomatoes:* halve them and remove the seeds. Grate them, cut side against the grater; you will be left holding the skin, which may be discarded.

8. *If using canned tomatoes:* Purée them in a food processor or pass them through the coarse holes of a vegetable mill.

7. Preheat the oven to 350°F.

9. Heat the oil and cook the onion gently, covered, for 10 minutes or until it is soft but not brown. Add the garlic and cook for another minute, add the pureed tomatoes, 1/4–1/2 cup of the reserved cooking liquid and season with salt and pepper. A pinch of sugar and a stick of cinnamon may also be added to the sauce at this stage. Allow the sauce to simmer for about 20 minutes, or until the ingredients blend.

10. Remove the sauce from the heat, add the parsley and pour it over the beans in the baking dish. (If you included a cinnamon stick in the sauce, discard it). Arrange the tomato slices over the beans and sprinkle them with salt, pepper and oregano.

11. Bake the dish, uncovered, for 50 minutes. Add a little of the reserved bean cooking liquid during baking if it begins to look dry, however, bear in mind that the resulting sauce should be thick and creamy.

12. Allow the dish to come to room temperature, during which time the beans will soak up a little more liquid from the sauce and the flavors will blend.

Serve at room temperature.

Soaking time: 1 hour or overnight   Yield: 8–12 servings as an appetizer
Preparation time: 1 hour
Cooking time: 2–3 hours

Savory Pastries
Kritsínia

4 1/4 cups all-purpose flour (or pastry flour)
4 teaspoons baking powder
1 teaspoon salt
3 teaspoons sugar
2 teaspoons mustard
1/4 teaspoon black pepper
1/4 teaspoon cayenne pepper
1 cup vegetable oil
1 1/2 cups orange juice or water

1. Preheat the oven to 400°F.

2. Combine all the dry ingredients in a bowl, add the oil and the orange juice and mix well. If the dough is sticky, add a little more flour.

3. Once you have a soft ball of dough lift it onto a floured surface and divide it into 2 halves. Working with one ball of dough at a time, roll it out to a rectangle about 1/4 inch thick and 20 inches long by 5 inches wide.

4. Using a sharp knife or a pizza wheel cut the dough at 1/2– 3/4 inch intervals producing about 30 five-inch lengths of dough. Transfer them to an un-oiled baking sheet twisting each piece once or twice along its length if you wish.

5. Bake them for 15 minutes, or until golden.

Transfer carefully to a rack to cool.

Preparation time 20 minutes
Baking time 15 minutes

Yield 60 pieces

Olive Bread
Eleópita

THIS IS MADE with olives from the island of Thassos. These are ripe, black olives which have been air-cured in salt. They are mild, not bitter, and have a wrinkled appearance. If they are not available locally, substitute the more widely available oil-cured black olives.

- **1 pound bread dough, store bought or home made (see recipe below)**
- **1 cup oil-cured (wrinkled) black olives**
- **4 tablespoons olive oil**
- **1 medium onion, grated or finely chopped in a food processor**
- **1 tablespoon finely chopped dill**
- **1 teaspoon sugar (optional)**

1. Slide a small, sharp knife lengthwise against the pit of each olive 3–4 times removing the flesh. Let the olive pieces fall into a small bowl; discard the pits.

2. Place the bread dough into a mixing bowl, add the olives, olive oil, onion and dill and knead them into the dough. This will seem messy and difficult at first, but if you lift the dough onto a lightly floured surface and pat it into a disc you can place any olives that are not yet incorporated into the dough on top of the disc and fold the edges into the centre to enclose them. A light sprinkling of flour makes this task easier.

3. Shape the dough into a round or oblong loaf and place it on a baking tray.

4. Cover the loaf with a cloth kitchen towel and allow it to rise in a warm place for about one hour.

5. Preheat the oven to 475°F during the second half of the rising time.

6. When the loaf has risen, place it in the oven and immediately reduce the heat to 425°F.

7. After 15 minutes reduce the heat to 350°F and continue to bake for another 30 minutes.

8. When the loaf is ready it will sound hollow when it is turned over and tapped firmly. Allow it to cool on a wire rack.

Preparation: 40 minutes
Rising and baking: 1 hour 45 minutes

Yield: 1 medium loaf

Homemade Bread Dough

2 cups all purpose or bread flour
1 envelope dried yeast
1/2 teaspoon salt

1. Dissolve the yeast in 1 cup of tepid water. Add a pinch of sugar and allow it to stand for 10–15 minutes until it produces bubbles.

2. Combine the salt with the flour and pour in the yeast mixture.

3. Mix the ingredients together until they form a soft mass. Lift this out onto a floured work surface and knead it for about 10 minutes. If it is sticky at first, add little sprinkles of flour; it will become smoother as you work. Do not add flour during the last 2–3 minutes of kneading.

4. Cover it and allow it to rise until it is doubled in size. (About 1 hour in a warm room.) Knead it gently for a minute and proceed with step 1 of the recipe for olive bread.

Preparation time: 30 minutes
Rising time: 1 hour

Yield: 1 pound dough

Garlic Bread

Psomí Yemistó me Skórdo

1 long crusty loaf of French or Italian bread
6–8 tablespoons margarine, at room temperature
3 cloves of garlic, peeled and crushed to a pulp
1 tablespoon finely chopped parsley

1. Preheat the oven to 425°F.

2. Slice the bread length-wise into two halves.

3. Beat the margarine until it is soft and light. Add the garlic and parsley and season with salt. Beat the mixture again.

4. Spread the two cut surfaces of the bread with the margarine mixture and clap them back together. Wrap the loaf in aluminum foil and bake for 15 minutes.

Preparation time: 15 minutes
Baking time: 15 minutes

Yield: 1 loaf of garlic bread

French Potatoes
Patátes Galikés

2 pounds small (1 1/2 inch) round potatoes
1/2 cup all-purpose flour
Oil for shallow frying

1. Wash the potatoes and boil them in their skins, until they are tender (15–20 minutes). Drain.

2. Put the flour in a bowl. As soon as the potatoes are cool enough to handle pull off their skins and immediately toss them in the flour so that they become evenly coated.

3. Heat 1/2 inch of oil in a sauté pan on medium-high heat. Add the potatoes and cook for 6–7 minutes, turning them once or twice, until they are crisp and golden. Sprinkle them generously with salt and pepper and serve hot.

Preparation time: 1 hour   Yield: 4–6 servings

Rice with Walnuts
Rízi me Karydia

3 tablespoons margarine
10 ounces (1 1/2 cups) rice
3 1/2 cups hot water
2 teaspoons salt
2 ounces (1/2 cup) coarsely chopped walnuts
Ground black pepper

1. Melt the margarine over medium heat, add the rice and stir for 3–4 minutes.

2. Add the water, salt and walnuts and a little ground black pepper. When the water boils, lower the heat and cover the saucepan.

3. Simmer gently for about 20 minutes until the rice is tender.

Preparation time 15 minutes   Yield 4–6 servings
Cooking time 20 minutes

Cypriot Potatoes
Patátes Kypriakés

3 1/2 **pounds medium sized, oblong potatoes**
3/4 **cup vegetable oil**
1 **cup dry breadcrumbs**

1. Peel the potatoes, cut them in half crosswise and place them cut side down on a baking tray.

2. With a sharp paring knife, cut a cross into the top of each potato half. Brush them with the oil and sprinkle with salt and the dry breadcrumbs.

3. Bake at 350°F for 1 hour, or until they are tender. Do not add water to the baking dish.

Preparation time 15 minutes
Cooking time: 1 hour

Yield: 6 servings as a side dish
(about 24 pieces)

Baked Potatoes
Patátes sto Foúrno

8 **small Russet potatoes (about 7 ounces each)**
1–2 **tablespoons olive oil**
Ground cumin
8 **tablespoons margarine**

1. Wash the potatoes, scrubbing them well. Dry and rub them with the olive oil.

2. Wrap each potato in aluminum foil. Cook them under the broiler for one hour, turning once. Check that they are tender by prodding them with a fork and if necessary continue to cook for a further 15 minutes. Alternatively, cook over charcoal for 35–45 minutes, or until tender.

3. Mix the margarine with salt, pepper and a few pinches of ground cumin. Open each foil-wrapped potato with a cross-shaped cut and place a little seasoned margarine inside each potato.

Preparation time: 15 minutes
Cooking time: 1 hour

Yield: 4 servings

Mixed Baked Vegetables
Lahaniká se Pílino Skévos me Kálymma

THE FLAVORS of the vegetables in this dish are emphasized with simple seasonings. In such a simple dish it is essential that the ingredients are at their best.

3 onions
1 small eggplant
3 carrots
2 leeks
2 large tomatoes
3 celery stalks
2 sweet peppers
Juice of 1 lemon

1. Preheat the oven to 450°F.

2. Peel the onions, eggplant and carrots and cut them into bite-size chunks.

3. Trim the leeks, wash them well and cut into bite-size logs.

4. Cut the tomatoes and the celery into bite-size pieces.

5. Trim the stalks, seeds and ribs from the peppers and cut them into bite-size pieces.

6. Place all the vegetables in a large pot or on a baking tray with sides and sprinkle them with the lemon juice. Season generously with salt and pepper and cover with a lid or with aluminum foil.

7. Bake for 1 hour.

Preparation time: 30 minutes
Baking time: 1 hour

Yield: 4 servings as an accompaniment

Onion Soup
Kremmydósoupa

2 large onions
5 tablespoons margarine
2 tablespoons flour
4 cups water
1/4 cup dry white wine
8 slices baguette
1–2 tablespoons brandy (optional)

1. Peel the onions, slice them finely and cook gently in four tablespoons of the margarine for about 20 minutes.

2. Add the flour and stir for a minute. Gradually stir in the water and bring to a boil then cover the soup, reduce the heat, and simmer for twenty minutes.

3. Add the wine and season with salt and pepper; simmer for 5 minutes.

4. Fry the bread slices in the remaining tablespoon of margarine and, optionally, sprinkle them with the brandy.

5. Serve the soup hot, topped with the fried bread.

Preparation time: 1 hour   Yield: 4 servings

Bean Soup
Fasólia Soúpa

A NATIONAL DISH of Greece, served with good, crusty bread, a handful of olives and perhaps some mixed pickled vegetables, this soup makes a hearty, and healthy, meal.

> **1 pound dried baby lima beans**
> **4–5 onions**
> **3–4 carrots**
> **2 celery stalks**
> **2–3 cloves of garlic**
> **1/2 cup finely chopped parsley**
> **1 cup olive oil**
> **4–5 ripe tomatoes** *or* **1 (14 ounce) can plum tomatoes**
> **1/2–1 teaspoon hot red pepper (optional)**

1. Sort the beans, discarding any foreign particles, and rinse them well.

2. *To soak overnight:* Put the beans in a large bowl, cover with cold water by about 3 inches, and set them aside in a corner of the kitchen to soak overnight or for about 8 hours.

The following day, drain and transfer the beans to a large cooking pot. Add 6 cups of fresh water to the pot.

To soak the same day: Put the beans in a large pot, cover with plenty of water and bring to the boil. Boil for 5 minutes and drain.

Put 7 cups of fresh water in the pot and bring it to the boil, turn off the heat, add the beans and cover the pot. Leave the beans to soak for 1 hour.

3. Turn the heat to medium and, as the beans begin to boil, prepare the vegetables.

4. Peel and finely chop the onions. Peel the carrots and slice them into coins. Wash the celery and slice it thinly. Peel and coarsely chop the garlic. Add all these to the pot.

5. Add the parsley and the olive oil.

6. *If using fresh tomatoes:* Wash the tomatoes, plunge them into boiling water for no more than a minute. Pull off the skins, chop them coarsely and add them to the beans in the pot.

If using canned tomatoes: Chop or purée the contents of the can and add to the pot.

8. Season with freshly ground black pepper, but don't add salt at this stage. If you like, add the optional

hot red pepper. Stir well.

9. Cover the pot and adjust the heat to a steady simmer. Cook (stirring occasionally) until the beans are tender and the liquid has become creamy and smooth. Add extra hot water if necessary.

This will take about 2 hours to cook; it is wise, however, to allow at least one extra hour before you plan to serve the soup. Cooking times for beans can vary tremendously according to the age and size of the beans, and this soup, as is the case for many bean dishes, only improves with reheating.

10. Season with salt and more pepper according to taste.

Soaking time: 1 hour 30 minutes or overnight Yield: 6 servings
Preparation time: 45 minutes
Cooking time: approximately 2 hours

Creamy Cauliflower Soup
Soúpa Kounoupídi

1 medium cauliflower
3 potatoes
Freshly grated nutmeg
3 tablespoons margarine
2 tablespoons flour
1/4 cup finely chopped parsley

1. Wash the cauliflower, separate it into small florets and discard the thick stems. Peel and quarter the potatoes. Boil the cauliflower and the potatoes in a large pot of lightly salted water for 20–25 minutes, until they are very tender. Drain, reserving the cooking liquid.

3. Purée the potatoes and the cauliflower with 1 cup of the reserved cooking liquid. A vegetable mill works well here; alternatively use a blender or food processor.

4. Melt the margarine in a saucepan; add the flour and cook, stirring, for 2–3 minutes over medium heat. Continue to stir, gradually adding two cups of the reserved cooking liquid and simmer until a smooth sauce results.

5. Combine this sauce with the puréed vegetables, stir the soup well and add salt, pepper and nutmeg to taste.

Serve the soup hot, sprinkled with finely chopped parsley.

Preparation time: 45 minutes

Yield: 4–5 servings

Cream of Mushroom Soup
Soúpa me Manitária

1 pound mushrooms
6–7 green onions
3/4 cup medium grain rice
1–2 tablespoons finely chopped dill
3 tablespoons tahini
3 tablespoons lemon juice

1. Wash and finely chop the mushrooms and the green onions. Cook them in a deep pot with 1/4 cup of water, stirring on medium high heat until they are softened, about 10 minutes.

2. Add 8 cups of water and the rice. Bring the soup to a boil and simmer, lid askew, until the rice is tender, about 20 minutes.

3. Add the dill and season to taste with salt and pepper. Cook for 2–3 minutes more and remove from the heat.

4. Beat the tahini in a small bowl with three tablespoons of tepid water and the lemon juice. Continue to stir, adding spoonfuls of the soup until the sauce is the consistency of a light cream.

5. Stir the tahini sauce into the soup. Do not boil the soup again because this would cause the tahini to curdle.

Preparation time: 45 minutes
Cooking time: 20 minutes

Yield: 6 servings

Tomato Soup
Tomatósoupa

CANNED TOMATOES are not given as an alternative ingredient here because this soup relies upon the fresh flavors of tomatoes and zucchini at the end of summer. To make croutons; remove the crust from some good bread and cut it into cubes. Fry these in a little olive oil, or toss with oil and bake at 350°F until golden.

> 3 green onions
> 1/2 cup olive oil
> 2 zucchini
> 2 pounds ripe tomatoes (about 6 medium)
> 4 potatoes
> 2 cloves of garlic
> 1 pinch sugar
> 2 bay leaves
> 3–4 tablespoons finely chopped parsley
> Bread for making croutons (optional)

1. Trim and finely chop the green onions. Cook them gently in the olive oil for 2–3 minutes.

2. Wash and slice the zucchini and add them to the onions, cook gently, stirring from time to time, until they begin to wilt.

3. Wash and quarter the tomatoes. Peel and quarter the potatoes. Add these to the pot, stir well and continue to cook for about 10 minutes.

4. Add 6 cups of water, the garlic cloves, crushed lightly and peeled, the sugar, bay leaves and salt and pepper. Cover the pot, bring it to the boil and adjust the heat until it simmers steadily. Cook for 40 minutes with the lid askew.

5. Remove and discard the bay leaves and purée the soup in a blender or with a vegetable mill.

Serve hot, sprinkled with the parsley and, if desired, accompanied by croutons.

Preparation time: 50 minutes
Cooking time: 40 minutes

Yield: 5–6 servings

Spinach Soup
Soúpa me Spanáki

SPINACH SOUP is at its best when the stems have been removed and discarded. For this reason it is not advisable to substitute frozen spinach in this recipe since this product, convenient though it is, always includes the stems with the leaves. Here is one recipe where baby spinach, often more readily available, will work well.

Always wash spinach very well; even if it looks clean it often harbors an alarming amount of soil and sand.

> 1½ **pounds fresh spinach (or 1 pound baby spinach)**
> **1 onion**
> **2 cloves of garlic**
> **6 tablespoons olive oil**
> **4 cups hot water**
> **Grated nutmeg**
> **¼ cup pine nuts**

1. Remove any tough stems from the spinach. Wash the spinach in a large bowl of cold water, drain and refill the bowl with fresh cold water. Repeat as necessary until the drained water runs clear.

2. Bring a large pan of water to the boil and add salt. Put the spinach in this and cook for 3 minutes (a little less if using baby spinach). Drain and press the spinach with the back of a wooden spoon in the colander to remove as much moisture as possible. Chop the spinach finely.

3. Peel and grate the onion and crush the garlic to a pulp. Alternatively, peel the onion and quarter it, peel the garlic and put both into a food processor. Process until finely chopped. Heat four tablespoons of the olive oil in a large pot, add the onion and garlic and cook gently for 10 minutes.

4. Add the spinach and stir for a minute. Add the water and season with freshly grated nutmeg, salt and pepper. Simmer the soup gently for 15–20 minutes.

5. Heat the remaining 2 tablespoons of oil in a small frying pan and sauté the pine nuts on medium heat for 1–2 minutes.

Serve the soup hot, sprinkled with the pine nuts.

Preparation time: 45 minutes   Yield: 4 servings

Italian Minestrone

Minestrone Italikí

4 ounces dried white beans (cannellini are traditional)
1/2 cup olive oil
2 onions
2 garlic cloves
1 cup dry red wine
1 teaspoon oregano
1 teaspoon dried basil
2 carrots, peeled and sliced
4 tomatoes
2–3 tablespoons finely chopped celery leaves
1/2 small cabbage, shredded (about 2 cups)
1/2 cup ditalini (Italian soup pasta) or broken vermicelli

1. Sort, rinse and soak the beans in cold water for about 8 hours.

2. Peel the onions, halve them lengthwise, lay them cut side down and slice them lengthwise to produce 'fingers'. Peel and slice the garlic. Heat the oil in a large pot, add the onions and garlic and cook gently, stirring occasionally, until the onions are soft, about 20 minutes.

4. Add the wine, oregano, basil, and 6 cups of water, bring this to a boil and add the soaked and drained beans. Cover and simmer gently for 1 1/2 – 2 hours, or until the beans are tender.

5. Boil several cups of water, place the tomatoes in the water for about a minute, after which transfer them to cold water. Slip off their skins and chop them finely. Add the tomatoes to the beans along with the sliced carrots. Season with salt and pepper. Simmer for 10 minutes.

7. Add the chopped celery leaves, shredded cabbage and the pasta. If there is insufficient water remaining to cook the pasta, add a little extra; the resulting dish should not however be at all watery. Cook until the cabbage and the pasta are tender, 20–30 minutes.

Serve the minestrone in wide, shallow bowls with good bread alongside.

Soaking time: 6–8 hours
Preparation time: 1 hour
Cooking time: 2–21/2 hours

Yield: 4 servings

Cream of Vegetable Soup
Soúpa me Tahíni

2 medium carrots
1 eggplant
3 medium potatoes
3 medium zucchini
1 celery stalk, preferably with leaves
2 sweet green peppers
1 leek
1 cup finely chopped cabbage
3 tablespoons finely chopped dill
3 tablespoons finely chopped parsley
1 cup broken vermicelli pasta, or medium grain rice
4 tablespoons tahini
3 tablespoons lemon juice

1. *Prepare the vegetables:* Wash and peel the carrots, eggplant, potatoes and zucchini. Wash the celery stalk. Rinse the peppers; remove the stems and seeds. Make a deep, length-wise cut in the leek and wash it under running water, separating the layers as you wash them to remove any grit. Cut all these into 1/2 inch dice.

2. Place the chopped vegetables and the herbs into a large pot and add 10 cups of water. Bring this to a boil and adjust the heat, with the lid askew, until the vegetables simmer steadily. Cook for 20 minutes.

3. Add the rice or the vermicelli and a teaspoon of salt, stir and continue to cook for another 20 minutes, or until the rice and vegetables are tender. Remove the pot from the heat.

4. In a small bowl, mix the tahini with the lemon juice and 3 tablespoons tepid water until it is smooth. Take a ladle-full of the liquid from the soup and add it slowly to the tahini sauce stirring the sauce as you do so.

5. Add the tahini sauce to the soup in a thin stream, stirring the soup continuously. Do not boil the soup after the tahini has been added. Season to taste with salt and freshly ground black pepper.

Preparation time: 40 minutes
Cooking time: 40 minutes

Yield: 6–8 servings

Carrot Salad
Karóta Saláda

IN GREEK CUISINE, a salad (*saláda*), refers to raw or cooked vegetables most usually dressed in olive oil. It is also used to refer to a spread or paste such as eggplant dip (*Melintsanosalata*), where the ingredients are ground to a smooth purée, traditionally using a mortar and pestle.

The Greek village salad (*horiatiki*), too familiar to have been included in the original Greek edition of this book, should be mentioned here: Tomatoes, cucumbers, onions, sweet peppers and olives, are cut into generously sized pieces, tossed in olive oil and lemon or vinegar and arranged casually in a large bowl. It is at its best prepared in summer when the ingredients are in season.

The following salad is a refreshing side which works well during the winter months. Prepare this in advance to allow time for the flavours to blend as the salad cools.

4 medium carrots
1 apple
Juice of 1/2 lemon (or to taste)
2–3 tablespoons orange juice
1/2 teaspoon grated lemon zest
1/2 teaspoon grated orange zest

1. Wash, peel and grate the carrots and the apple.

2. Add the remaining ingredients, season with salt and mix the salad until it is well combined.

3. Refrigerate for 1–2 hours before serving.

Preparation time: 20 minutes
Refrigeration time: 1–2 hours

Yield: 3 cups salad

Zucchini Salad

Kolokythákia Saláda

Small zucchini are tender and delicious when prepared as a salad dish.

2 pounds small zucchini (about 1 1/2 inch diameter)
2 tablespoons olive oil
1 onion, peeled
Juice of 1 lemon

Dressing and garnish:
1/4 cup olive oil
Juice of 1/2 lemon
1 small onion
2 tablespoons finely chopped dill

1. Trim and peel the zucchini. Place them in a pot with 1–2 cups of water, the oil, onion, lemon juice, and salt and pepper.

2. Simmer them with the lid askew until they are tender (this will take between 15 and 20 minutes). Do not allow them to overcook.

3. Discard the onion and transfer the zucchini to a serving platter.

4. Beat the oil and lemon and pour it over the zucchini. Turn the zucchini to coat them in the dressing. Sprinkle with salt and pepper and allow to cool to room temperature.

5. Slice the onion very thinly and spread it over the zucchini. Sprinkle with the dill to serve.

Preparation time: 20 minutes
Cooking/cooling time: 45 minutes

Yield: 6–8 servings

Celery Root Salad
Sélino Saláda

A REFRESHING SALAD whose main ingredient is in season in winter when many salad vegetables are not at their best. Smaller celery roots (celeriac) are the most tender and most suited to eating raw. If this is not available, or if it is old and spongy, try substituting 7–8 tender celery stalks, strings removed and finely sliced.

1 small celery root
1 apple
Juice of 1 lemon

Dressing and garnish:
3 tablespoons olive oil
1 tablespoon vinegar
1/4 cup coarsely chopped walnuts
1–2 tablespoons young celery leaves

1. Wash the celery root, take slices off the top and base, and cut it in half. Place it, cut side down, on a chopping board and slice off all the brown skin. Grate it on the coarse side of a box-grater and toss with the lemon juice to reduce browning.

2. Wash, peel and grate the apple.

3. Add the apple to the grated celery root, season with salt and freshly ground black pepper and mix well. Cover and refrigerate for 1 hour.

4. Beat the oil with the vinegar and add it to the salad, tossing well. Allow to stand for half an hour at room temperature before serving.

Serve garnished with the coarsely chopped walnuts and celery leaves.

Preparation time: 30 minutes
Standing time: 1 hour 30 minutes

Yield: 4 servings

French Salad
Gallikí Saláda

3 cups eggless mayonnaise, store-bought or prepared according to recipe on page 37
2 tablespoons ketchup
1 pound boiling potatoes
2 medium carrots
2 stalks celery
1 cup frozen peas
2 tablespoons finely chopped parsley
2 small apples, peeled and diced
3/4 cup diced pickled gherkins

1. *If using homemade mayonnaise:* Prepare the mayonnaise according to the recipe on page 37, combine it with the ketchup and put it in the refrigerator to cool.

If using store-bought mayonnaise: Combine it with the ketchup.

2. Boil the potatoes whole, in their skins, until they are tender (about 35 minutes, or less if they are small). Drain them, and when they are cool enough to handle, slip off their skins. Dice them, place them in a bowl and set aside to cool.

3. Peel the carrots and quarter them length-wise. Chop the carrots into small pieces. Halve the celery stalks length-wise and chop into small pieces.

4. Put the carrots in a pan of boiling water and set a timer for 5 minutes. After 5 minutes add the celery, peas and parsley and cook for another 3 minutes, or until the vegetables are just tender. Do not over-cook them. Drain them and add to the potatoes.

5. Add the apples and the gherkins to the vegetable mixture and season with a little freshly grated black pepper. Add the mayonnaise and stir carefully to combine.

6. Chill the salad for at least 30 minutes before serving.

Preparation time: 1 hour

Yield: 8 servings as an appetizer or side dish

Refrigeration time: 30–60 minutes

Eggless Mayonnaise
Mayonéza

1/2 **cup flour**
2 **cups water**
2 **teaspoons white vinegar**
2 **teaspoons sugar**
1/2 **teaspoon powdered mustard**
1 **teaspoon salt**
1 **cup vegetable oil**
2 **tablespoons lemon juice**

1. Heat the flour and water in a small saucepan beating with a wire whisk until the mixture simmers and becomes thick and smooth. Remove it from the heat and beat it occasionally as it cools to prevent the formation of a skin.

2. Put the cooled flour and water mixture in the bowl of a food processor (or electric mixer) and add the vinegar, sugar, mustard and salt. Turn the processor on and add the vegetable oil and the lemon juice alternately in small quantities until they are incorporated and the mayonnaise is smooth and creamy. Taste and adjust the seasoning.

3. Cool in the refrigerator for at least 30 minutes before serving.

Preparation time: 30 minutes
Refrigeration time: 30 minutes

Yield: 3 cups

Potato Salad
Patátes Saláda

WAXY, BOILING potatoes work well in salads because they have a smooth tender texture when boiled but they do not become powdery and break apart. Avoid Russets (baking potatoes) for this very problem.

Plan to eat this on the day it is made; potato dishes of any kind are spoiled by refrigeration. The flavours of the dressing are better absorbed when the potatoes are still a little warm. Serve this dish when it is still slightly warm, or at room temperature.

2 pounds boiling potatoes
1/2 cup olive oil
Juice of 1 lemon
1 tablespoon mustard
1 small onion, thinly sliced
3–4 tablespoons finely chopped parsley

1. Wash the potatoes and boil them, in their skins, for 30–40 minutes, or until they are tender but not overcooked. (If your potatoes are the small, new kind then they will require less time to cook). Drain.

2. Pull off their skins while they are still warm and cut them into bite-size cubes. Place in a serving dish.

3. With a wire whisk, combine the olive oil, lemon juice and mustard. Season this dressing with salt and pepper and pour it over the potatoes. Toss gently.

4. Top the potatoes with the onion slices and sprinkle with the parsley to serve.

Preparation time: 50 minutes

Yield: 4 servings

Rice Salad
Rizi Saláda

IN GREECE rice dishes are sometimes packed into a decorative pan (a brioche pan or a bundt pan), and turned out onto a plate to serve. This is remarkably easy to do and this dish looks particularly attractive when it is presented in this way.

> **1 cup long grain rice**
> **2-3 carrots**
> **1/2 pound green beans**
> **1/2 pound frozen peas**
> **3–4 green onions**
> **1 (15 ounce) can corn**
> **1 sweet red pepper**
>
> **Sauce:**
> **4 tablespoons tahini**
> **4 tablespoons water**
> **Juice of 1/2 lemon**

1. Bring a large pot of water to a boil and add two teaspoons of salt. Add the rice and boil until it is tender, about 12 minutes. Drain the rice and leave it to cool.

2. Peel the carrots and halve them lengthwise, chop them into 1/2-inch lengths. Boil in salted water for 3–4 minutes. Wash the beans and chop them into 1/2-inch lengths, add them to the carrots and continue cooking for another 3–4 minutes. Finally add the peas and cook for a further 2 minutes. Drain the vegetables and leave them to cool.

3. Finely chop the green onions. Drain the corn. Wash, core and seed the pepper and cut it into 1/2 inch dice.

4. Add the prepared vegetables to the rice. Taste and adjust the seasoning.

5. Prepare the sauce: Beat the tahini together with the lemon juice and add the water whilst continuing to beat. Season to taste with salt and pepper. The resulting sauce should have the consistency of thin honey.

Serve the rice at room temperature with the sauce poured over it.

Preparation time: 40 minutes   Yield: 4 servings

Pasta with Olives and Tomatoes
Makarónia me Eliés kai Tomátes

12 ounces ziti pasta (or similar)
3 tablespoons olive oil
1 stick (4 ounces) margarine
1 clove of garlic
4 ripe tomatoes
3 ounces black olives, pitted
3 tablespoons finely chopped parsley
1 can corn (15 ounces)
1 tablespoon finely chopped celery leaves

1. Boil the pasta in plenty of salted water with one tablespoonful of the oil for the time given on the packet. Drain and place in a serving bowl.

2. Peel and crush the garlic clove to a pulp. Heat the margarine and add the garlic and the remaining 2 tablespoons of oil, stir once or twice and remove from the heat. Pour this over the pasta and stir to coat the pasta evenly.

3. Cut the tomatoes into bite-size pieces and add them to the pasta with the olives, parsley and celery. Drain the corn and add it to the pasta. Toss the pasta gently, taste and adjust the seasoning, and serve warm or at room temperature.

Preparation time: 30 minutes   Yield: 4 servings

Orzo in Tomato Sauce

Kritharáki me Saltsa

PASTA, made by hand and dried for the winter, is found in dozens of varieties in villages throughout Greece. One of these is the rice-like *kritharáki* pasta which is made by pinching off tiny pieces of dough and rolling them between the fingers. The Italian soup pasta called *orzo* makes a good, easily obtainable substitute.

> **2 pounds ripe tomatoes, or 2 (14 ounce) cans plum tomatoes**
> **6 tablespoons olive oil**
> **2 cloves of garlic, finely chopped**
> **1 tablespoon finely chopped parsley**
> **1 sprig basil, leaves detached and finely chopped**
> **1/2 cup dry white wine**
> **1 pound orzo pasta**

1. *If using fresh tomatoes:* Skin, seed and finely chop them.

If using canned tomatoes: Use both juice and tomatoes, which should be chopped finely.

2. Heat the oil in a large pot and add the garlic and the parsley. Cook gently for about 30 seconds; do not allow the garlic to take color. Add the tomatoes and basil, 2 teaspoons of salt (less if your canned tomatoes have added salt) and some freshly ground black pepper.

3. Simmer the sauce, uncovered, for about 10 minutes, add the wine and, when it returns to the boil, add the orzo and 1 cup of hot water (1 1/4 cups if cooking with canned tomatoes), and stir well.

4. Cook with the lid askew on medium-low heat for about 12–15 minutes (calculate this by adding 3–4 minutes to the cooking time given on the package). Stir frequently to prevent sticking and add extra water as needed. When the liquid has been absorbed the orzo should be just tender.

5. Remove the pot from the heat, drape a cloth napkin or tea towel over it, cover with the lid and allow to stand for 20-30 minutes.

Serve hot.

Preparation time: 30 minutes   Yield: 4–5 servings
Cooking time: 45-55 minutes

Penne with Tahini Sauce
Makaronáki koftó me Saltsa apo Tahíni

TAHINI SAUCE makes a simple and unusual dressing for pasta.

> **1 pound penne, or similar pasta**
> **Sauce:**
> **6 tablespoons tahini**
> **2 tablespoons lemon juice**
> **2 cloves of garlic, crushed to a pulp**

1. Bring a large pot of water to the boil, add a tablespoon of salt and, when it returns to the boil, add the pasta. Cook the pasta for the length of time given on the box.

2. Prepare the sauce as the pasta cooks: Place the tahini in a small bowl, add the lemon juice, garlic, salt and a little freshly ground pepper and stir well until it is smooth.

3. When the pasta is tender, drain, reserving two cups of the cooking water.

4. Add the reserved water to the tahini mixture a little at a time, stirring all the while, until you have a rather thin but creamy sauce. Add extra water if the sauce is thick, otherwise it will not make a suitable dressing for pasta.

5. Toss the pasta in the sauce and serve immediately.

Preparation time: 20 minutes   Yield: 5–6 small servings

Pasta with Olives
Makarónia me Eliés

1 cup black olives
1 medium onion
1/2 cup olive oil
3 medium tomatoes
1 sweet green pepper
1/2 cup white wine
Pinch dried rosemary
1 pound pasta of choice

1. Use a sharp paring knife to take 3 or 4 slivers from each olive (sliding the knife lengthwise against the pit), discard the pits. Cover the olive pieces with cold water and bring them to the boil. Simmer for 5 minutes. Drain.

2. Peel and finely chop the onion. Heat the oil in a medium pot, add the onion and cook gently for about 10 minutes, or until the onion is soft.

3. Bring a large pot of water to the boil. Add the tomatoes and, after one minute, remove them with a slotted spoon to a bowl of cold water. Pull off their skins and chop them into small pieces. Reserve the hot water for cooking the pasta.

4. Wash the pepper. Remove the stem and seeds and chop it finely.

5. Add the pepper and the tomatoes to the onion. Simmer, uncovered, for 15 minutes.

6. Add the wine and rosemary and season with salt and pepper (take care not to add too much salt at this point because the olives may be salty).

7. Simmer the sauce, stirring occasionally, for another 10–15 minutes. Add the olives and simmer for 5 minutes. Taste and adjust the seasoning as necessary.

8. Add salt to the pot of hot water, return it to the boil and cook the pasta for the time given on the package. Drain.

9. Pour the sauce over the pasta, toss gently and serve immediately.

Preparation time: 40 minutes
Cooking time: 40 minutes

Yield: 4–5 servings

Vegetable Pasta Bake
Pastitsio me Manitária

Vegetable Sauce:
1/2 pound frozen peas
2 medium carrots
1 large onion
1/4 cup olive oil
1 pound mushrooms
3 cloves of garlic
1 pound tomatoes, skinned and finely chopped,
   or 1 (14-ounce) can plum tomatoes, finely chopped
1 tablespoon finely chopped basil leaves
1 teaspoon dried oregano

Béchamel Sauce:
9 tablespoons margarine
11 tablespoons flour
5 cups hot water
   or 3 cups of water plus 2 cups unsweetened, plain soymilk, heated
1/4 teaspoon grated nutmeg
4 tablespoons finely chopped parsley

To Construct the Dish:
1 pound eggless lasagne pasta
1 tablespoon salt
3–4 tablespoons oil
9 black olives, pitted

1. *To prepare the vegetable sauce:* Boil the peas in salted water for 2–3 minutes, until almost tender, drain and set aside.

2. Peel and finely chop the carrots and the onion. Alternatively, quarter the onion and the carrots and place them in the bowl of a food processor. Pulse until they are finely chopped. Cook them gently in a medium pot in 1/4 cup of oil, covered, for about 10 minutes, or until the onion is soft.

3. Wash and finely chop the mushrooms and the garlic and add them to the onion mixture. Stir well and continue to cook on low heat, stirring occasionally, for 10 minutes.

4. Add the tomatoes, basil and oregano and season with salt and pepper. Simmer this mixture on medium heat, stirring occasionally, until the excess liquid evaporates. Do not cover the pot. You should have about 4 cups of sauce.

5. *To prepare the béchamel:* Melt the margarine add the flour and stir over low heat for one or two minutes. Add the hot water or water and soy milk, beating with a wire whisk. Cook until the sauce thickens then remove it from the heat, season with nutmeg and salt and stir in the finely chopped parsley. This will make about 5 cups of sauce.

6. Preheat the oven to 400°F.

7. *To construct the dish:* Bring a large pot of water to a boil, add the salt and 1 tablespoon of oil and cook the pasta until it is tender, do not overcook. Drain and rinse in plenty of cold water, then toss in two-three tablespoons of oil to prevent the pasta from sticking together.

8. Grease a 12 inch by 10 inch baking pan, which should be at least 3 inches deep, and spread 1/2 cup of béchamel sauce over the base of the pan. Place one fourth of the pasta in the pan, spread about 1 1/2 cups of the vegetable sauce over it and scatter a handful of the peas over this. Spread about 1/2 cup of the béchamel sauce over this layer. Repeat these layers two more times, finishing with a final layer of pasta and a thick layer (you should have about 3 cups remaining) of béchamel sauce.

9. Decorate the surface of the béchamel with the black olives and bake for 25–30 minutes.

Allow to stand for 20–30 minutes before serving.

Preparation time: 1 hour   Yield: 6 servings
Baking time: 30 minutes
Standing time: 30 minutes

Note: This recipe may also be made with the type of lasagne pasta known as 'no boil'. In this case, skip step 7 and proceed to construct the dish as described in step 8, using the dry pasta sheets.

Spinach Pie
Spanakópita

PHYLLO DOUGH can be purchased, frozen, at many supermarkets and at Greek or Middle Eastern food stores. If you intend to use it within a day or two, put it into the refrigerator when you get home. This way it will be defrosted and ready to use. It should not be opened until necessary and, once it is opened, any dough that you are not working with must remain covered to prevent drying. The sheets of dough in this recipe are not neatly stacked but are pleated and arranged casually; this results in a lighter, less compact pie.

> **2 - 2 1/2 pounds fresh spinach (not baby spinach)**
> **_or_ 2 pounds frozen chopped spinach**
> **1 cup olive oil**
> **3 medium leeks**
> **2 carrots (optional)**
> **1 onion (optional)**
> **2–3 tablespoons finely chopped dill**
> **1 tablespoon lemon juice**
> **1 pound phyllo pastry dough, defrosted**
> **1 six ounce bottle soda water**

1. Put a pot of water on to boil for cooking the spinach.

2. *If using fresh spinach:* Trim and discard any tough stems. Working in batches, place the spinach in a large bowl of cold water, swish it around then lift it out. Drain and repeat as necessary, until no more traces of soil or grit are to be seen in the water as the spinach is lifted out.

Cook it in boiling water until it is tender, this will take 3-5 minutes, depending on the spinach. Drain it through a colander and press it with the back of a large wooden spoon to remove the excess moisture. Chop the spinach finely.

If using frozen spinach: Add it to the boiling water and cook for one minute then drain it through a colander. Press the spinach with the back of a large wooden spoon to remove the excess water.

3. Wash, trim and thinly slice the leeks. Heat 1/2 cup of the oil in a large frying pan and cook the leeks gently for about 10 minutes, until they are tender. (If you wish to include the onion and carrots they should be peeled, finely chopped and cooked with the leeks).

4. Add the spinach, dill and lemon juice. Season generously with salt and pepper. Stir well and remove

the pan from the heat.

5. Preheat the oven to 350°F.

6. Oil a large (12x18 inches, with 1 inch deep sides) baking tray.

7. Unwrap and unfold the phyllo dough. Use a pastry brush to spread a little of the remaining oil over the first pastry sheet and place it in the baking tray. Repeat this with the following five or six sheets of dough, do not worry about creases and wrinkles but simply cover the base of the tray evenly.

8. Spread the next sheet of pastry with 2–3 tablespoons of the spinach mixture. The spinach will not be evenly spread but the oil from the filling mixture should cover much of the pastry sheet. Make a couple of deep pleats in it before lifting it into the baking tray.

9. Repeat this process with most of the remaining pastry dough, arranging the pleated pieces randomly, but filling the tray evenly. It is not necessary to brush these layers with oil; the oil in the spinach mixture is sufficient.

10. The last 5–6 sheets of phyllo dough should be brushed with oil and stacked on top to cover the pie. Use a sharp knife to score the pie into 12 serving pieces.

11. Mix the bottle of soda water with any remaining olive oil and pour it over the pie.

12. Bake for about 1 hour, or until golden.

Preparation time: 45 minutes   Yield: one 12x18 inch pie (12 small pieces)
Baking time: 1 hour

Tomato Pizza
Tomatópita

THE TOMATOES used in this recipe should be red and ripe, at their peak and full of flavor. To avoid making the pizza crust wet, be sure to drain them well.

Crust:
1 envelope dry yeast
11/4 cups warm water
1/2 teaspoon sugar
3 cups flour
1 teaspoon salt
1 tablespoon olive oil

Topping:
4 large ripe but firm tomatoes
1–2 teaspoons oregano
5–6 cloves of garlic
4 tablespoons olive oil

1. *To prepare the dough:* Put 1/2 cup of warm water in a small bowl and add the yeast, sugar and a sprinkle of flour. Stir and let stand in a warm place for about 10 minutes, until bubbles appear on the surface.

2. Put the flour and salt into a mixing bowl and make a well in the centre of the flour. Pour the yeast mixture and the tablespoon of olive oil into the well. Add the remaining 3/4 cup of warm water gradually whilst stirring, then kneading, until a ball of dough is formed.

3. Knead for several minutes on a floured work surface until the dough is smooth and elastic. Cover it with a damp kitchen towel and let it rest in a warm place for about an hour, until it is doubled in size.

4. *To prepare the topping:* Wash the tomatoes and cut them in half horizontally. Cut out the woody stems with a paring knife and scoop out the seeds. Cut them horizontally into 1/4 inch slices and place on paper towels to drain any excess moisture.

5. Put the tomato slices into a bowl and sprinkle with salt, oregano and 2 tablespoons of the olive oil. Toss gently until they are evenly coated.

6. Peel and slice the garlic cloves and set them aside.

7. *To assemble the pizza:* Knead the dough briefly and place it in the centre of an oiled pizza pan (14-inch diameter). Press it with your fingers until it covers the base of the pan; if the dough resists let it stand for five minutes to relax, then try again.

8. Preheat the oven to 425°F and let the dough rest for 30 minutes.

9. Scatter the garlic over the dough and arrange the tomato slices to cover the entire surface. Drizzle with the remaining 2 tablespoons of olive oil and sprinkle with a little salt, pepper and oregano.

10. Bake the pizza for about 40 minutes. Carefully lift the edge of the pie to check that the underside is no longer soft and doughy.

Serve warm or at room temperature.

Preparation time: 40 minutes   Yield: one 14-inch pizza
Rising time: 11/2 hours
Baking time: 40 minutes

Vegetable Pizza
Pitsa

Crust:
1 pound all-purpose flour
1 envelope dried yeast
1 1/2 cups warm water
1 1/2 teaspoons salt
3/4 teaspoon sugar
1 teaspoon olive oil

Topping:
3 large tomatoes
1/2 pound mushrooms
1 sweet green pepper
6–8 black olives
2 tablespoons mustard
2 tablespoons tomato ketchup
2 tablespoons capers
3 tablespoons olive oil
1 teaspoon oregano

1. *Prepare the dough:* Dissolve the yeast in the water, stir in 1 cup of the flour and leave the mixture to stand in a warm place for about 20 minutes, until the surface of the mixture is covered with bubbles.

2. Put the remaining flour in a bowl, make a well in the centre into which pour the yeast mixture, salt and sugar. Stir and gather the ingredients into a ball and knead this vigorously for 6–7 minutes.

3. Put the teaspoon of oil into a bowl, turn the dough in it to coat and leave to stand in a warm place, covered with a clean towel, until doubled in volume, about one hour.

4. *Prepare the topping while the dough rises:* Place the tomatoes in a bowl and pour boiling water over them, after 3–4 minutes plunge them into cold water. Remove their skins and cut them in half horizontally. Remove their seeds and slice them. Put the tomato slices in a colander to drain.

5. Wash and slice the mushrooms. Remove the stem and seeds from the pepper and slice it. Use a paring knife to cut slivers from the olives; discard the pits.

6. Preheat the oven to 400°F when the dough is almost doubled in volume.

7. *Construct the pizza:* Knead the dough briefly to deflate it and place it in a large oiled baking tray (12x18 inches), with raised sides. Press the dough with your fingertips until it covers the base of the tray; if the dough resists, allow it to rest for 10 minutes and try again.

8. Mix the mustard with the ketchup and spread this mixture over the dough. Arrange the tomato slices over this and add the olive pieces. Add the mushrooms, capers and green pepper. Sprinkle the pizza with the olive oil and oregano, salt and freshly ground black pepper.

9. Bake at 400°F for 15 minutes. Then reduce the heat to 350°F and continue to bake the pizza for 25–30 minutes.

Serve the pizza hot.

Rising time: 1 hour   Yield: 8 pizza slices
Preparation time: 45 minutes
Baking time: 45 minutes

VEGETABLE DISHES

LEGUMES

STUFFED DISHES

SECTION TWO

Artichokes in Dill and Lemon Sauce
Anginóres Laderés

12 fresh Globe artichokes, *or* 12 frozen artichoke hearts
3 lemons
1 cup olive oil
1 large onion, grated or chopped very finely in a food processor
1 tablespoon all-purpose flour
1/4 cup finely chopped dill
3–4 carrots, peeled and sliced
1 pound frozen peas
5-6 pearl onions, peeled

1. *To prepare fresh artichokes:* Have ready a bowl of water into which squeeze the juice of one of the lemons. The basic principle here is that the green parts of the artichoke are tough and inedible; if there seems to be a lot of waste, bear in mind that this is, after all, a thistle plant, which happens to have a delicious interior. The leaves of the artichoke should be snapped off (leaving only the pale, tender base of each leaf), until only the very pale leaves remain at the centre. Trim these off just above the base and at the very centre you will see a core of small leaves whose points curl inwards. These are prickly and should be pulled out and discarded. The fuzzy central choke will now be visible and should be scraped out using a small spoon. Lastly, use a paring knife to trim (but not remove) the stem and peel off the remaining green exterior from the stem and base of the artichoke, along with any green remains of the discarded outer leaves. Place the heart of the artichoke into the acidulated water to limit discoloration.

If using frozen artichoke hearts: Begin with step 2.

2. Peel and grate the onion, or chop it very finely in a food processor. Peel and chop the carrots into thick coins. Heat the oil in a braising pan (substitute a large, fairly deep frying pan with a lid), and add the grated onion. Sauté the onion until it wilts, then add the flour and stir it for a minute.

3. Add 2 cups of water, the dill, carrots and peas with salt and pepper to taste. Stir well. Nestle the artichokes (stems pointing up) in the pea and carrot bed. Squeeze the juice of the remaining 2 lemons into the pan and add the pearl onions.

4. Cover the pan with aluminum foil in which make a hole to allow the steam to escape. Place the lid over the foil and simmer the artichokes on medium-low heat until they are tender, 30–45 minutes.

Preparation time: 45 minutes
Cooking time: 45 minutes

Yield: 4 servings

Braised Celery Root
Selináto

CHOOSE CELERY ROOTS (also known as celeriac) that are firm with no hint of sponginess.

> **2 medium-large celery roots**
> **1 onion**
> **1/2 cup olive oil**
> **2 tablespoons finely chopped celery leaves**
> **Juice of 1 lemon**
> **2 tablespoons cornstarch**

1. Cut a slice off the top and base of each celery root and cut them length wise in half. Place the pieces, cut side down, on your cutting board and use a sharp knife to cut off all the brown skin. Cut each piece lengthwise into four wedges.

2. Peel and grate the onion, or chop it very finely in a food processor. Choose a pot that will subsequently accommodate the celery root wedges. Heat the oil in the pot and add the onion. Cook gently for 5–10 minutes.

3. Add the celery roots and leaves, half of the lemon juice, salt and pepper and about 1 1/2 cups of water. Simmer, covered, for 30–45 minutes, or until the celery roots are tender. Add additional water if it becomes too dry.

4. Transfer the celery roots to a serving dish with a slotted spoon.

5. Dissolve the cornstarch in the remaining lemon juice and add this to the cooking liquid in the pan. Stir and heat the sauce until it simmers and thickens. Adjust the seasoning if necessary.

6. Pour this sauce over the roots and serve hot.

Preparation time: 30 minutes   Yield: 4 servings
Cooking time: 30–45 minutes

Spinach Rice
Spanakórizo

SPINACH RICE is nourishing and delicious. This unusual version replaces the more common oil and tomato base with a tahini cream sauce. When cooking with fresh spinach it is essential to wash it well otherwise the resulting dish will be gritty and unpleasant.

> **2 pounds fresh spinach,** *or* **1 pound frozen spinach**
> **5-6 green onions, finely chopped**
> **1/4 cup finely chopped dill**
> **1 cup long grain rice**
> **2 teaspoons salt**
> **3 tablespoons lemon juice**
> **4 tablespoons tahini**

1. *If using fresh spinach*: Discard the tough stems. Place the spinach in a large bowl and wash it in several changes of cold water until the water in the bowl runs clear leaving no trace of soil or grit. Cook the spinach for 3-5 minutes in boiling water, drain and chop finely.

If using frozen spinach: Defrost and chop finely.

2. Put the onions in a pot with 1/4 cup of water and cook for a few minutes until softened, add the spinach and 3 cups of water. Bring the water to the boil, stir in the rice and 1 teaspoon of salt.

3. Cover the pot and simmer for 15 minutes. Stir in the dill and continue to simmer for a further five minutes, or until the rice is tender.

4. In a small bowl, dilute the tahini with two tablespoons of tepid water and the lemon juice. Beat this mixture whilst adding spoonfuls of the cooking liquid from the pot. When the tahini sauce is smooth stir it into the spinach rice. Season to taste with salt and pepper and serve hot.

Preparation time: 45 minutes   Yield: 4 servings

Braised Green Beans
Fasoulákia Yiahní

21/2 pounds fresh green beans, *or* 2 pounds frozen
1 cup olive oil
1 large onion
3 large ripe tomatoes, *or* 1 (14 ounce) can plum tomatoes
2 sweet green peppers
3 cloves of garlic
1/4 cup finely chopped parsley

1. *To prepare fresh green beans:* Snap off the ends, pulling away any strings as you work. Wash them and cut them into halves if they are very long.

If using frozen beans: Begin at step 2.

2. Peel and grate the onion, or chop it very finely in a food processor. Heat the olive oil in a large pot and sauté the onion on medium heat for 5–7 minutes.

3. *If using fresh tomatoes:* Wash them and cut them horizontally into halves. Use the coarse side of a box grater to grate the tomato halves, cut side first. Discard the skins, which will be left in your hand.

4. *If using canned tomatoes:* Chop them finely.

5. Wash, trim and finely chop the peppers. Add the tomatoes and peppers to the pot and simmer for 5–10 minutes.

6. Add the beans and 1 cup of water. Stir well, then cover and allow the beans to simmer for about an hour (45 minutes if you are using frozen beans). If the sauce becomes too dry, add sufficient extra water to cook the beans, however the finished sauce must not be at all watery.

7. Peel and slice the garlic. Add the garlic, parsley, a pinch of sugar and salt and pepper and continue to cook for 15 minutes, by which time the sauce should be reduced and thick.

Adjust the seasoning and serve hot or at room temperature.

Preparation time: 45 minutes
Cooking time: 1 hour 15 minutes

Yield: 4–5 servings

Leeks and Potatoes with Tahini Sauce
Prássa me Patátes

Leeks sometimes hold soil and grit between the layers of their stems. Make a lengthwise slit (about 1/2-inch deep) along the stem and separate the layers as you wash them.

This requires little more than crusty bread, a handful of olives and some raw or pickled vegetables to make a hearty meal.

1 large onion
1 pound potatoes
2 pounds leeks
1 cup canned puréed tomatoes (about one 14 ounce can)
2–3 carrots
2 sweet peppers
3 tablespoons tahini
Juice of 1 lemon

1. Peel and wash the vegetables. Cut the leeks into 2-inch logs, quarter the potatoes, cut the peppers into bite size pieces and the carrots into coins.

2. Peel the onion and grate it, or chop it very finely in a food processor. Place the onion in a large pot with 1/4 cup of water and cook, stirring, until it wilts.

3. Add the puréed tomatoes, potatoes, leeks, carrots, peppers and 1/2 cup of water. Place the lid on the pot and turn the heat to medium-low. Cook the vegetables for 45 minutes, or until they are tender.

4. Beat the tahini with the lemon juice and two or three tablespoons of tepid water.

5. Transfer the cooked vegetables to a serving bowl with a slotted spoon and blend the remaining cooking liquid into the tahini mixture.

Pour the sauce over the vegetables and serve hot.

Preparation time: 30 minutes   Yield: 4 servings
Cooking time: 45 minutes

Mushrooms with Onions and Peppers
Manitária me Kremmydákia

1 pound mushrooms
2 sweet green peppers
15 pearl onions (about 4 ounces)
2 crab apples (substitute 1 Granny Smith)
1/2 cup olive oil
2 ounces margarine
1 tablespoon yellow mustard
2 tablespoons ketchup
1 tablespoon oregano
1/2 cup finely chopped parsley

1. Wash the mushrooms and halve or quarter them as necessary to make bite-sized pieces. Seed and chop the peppers. Peel the onions. Peel and slice the apples into wedges.

2. Heat the oil with the margarine and sauté the mushrooms, peppers and onions for several minutes.

3. Add the remaining ingredients and season with salt and pepper.

4. Cook at a steady simmer until the mushrooms are tender, about 30 minutes.

Serve hot with bread, rice or plain boiled potatoes.

Preparation time: 20 minutes
Cooking time: 30 minutes

Yield: 4 small servings

Peas and Lettuce
Bizélia

2 onions
6–7 green onions
3/4 cup olive oil
1 small lettuce
2 pounds frozen peas,
4-5 tomatoes, *or* 1 (14 ounce) can plum tomatoes
3 tablespoons finely chopped dill

1. Peel and grate the onions, or chop them very finely in a food processor. Wash, trim and thinly slice the green onions. Heat the olive oil in a large pot and cook both types of onion for 3–4 minutes.

2. *If using fresh tomatoes:* Cut them in half horizontally and grate them, cut side against the coarse holes of a four-sided grater. Discard the skins.

If using canned tomatoes: Purée them in a food processor or blender (or chop them very finely).

3. Wash and finely chop the lettuce. Add this to the pot with the peas, tomatoes and dill.

4. Add sufficient water to allow the peas to move freely, without swimming in the liquid. This will be between 1 and 2 cups, depending on the amount of liquid in the tomatoes. Season with salt and pepper.

5. Simmer, covered, for about 30 minutes. When the peas are cooked the sauce should be reduced and not at all watery.

Serve with rice if desired.

Preparation time: 30 minutes
Cooking time: 30 minutes

Yield: 4 servings

Mushroom Goulash
Manitária Goúlas

2 pounds mushrooms
1 sweet green pepper
4 onions
4 tomatoes, *or* 1 (14 ounce) can plum tomatoes
1 cup olive oil
1 tablespoon ground sweet paprika
1/4 cup finely chopped parsley
2 pounds potatoes, boiled, to serve

1. Put a pot of water on to boil if you will be skinning fresh tomatoes.

2. Wash the mushrooms and cut them into thick slices. Wash, seed and finely chop the pepper. Peel and grate the onions, or peel and quarter them and chop them very finely in a food processor.

3. *To prepare fresh tomatoes:* Place them in the boiling water for one minute, skin and seed them. Chop the flesh into small pieces.

To use canned tomatoes: Chop them into small pieces.

4. Heat the oil in a large pot and cook the onion and the pepper for 2 minutes, add the mushrooms and continue to cook for another 2 minutes.

5. Add the tomatoes and paprika, season with salt and black pepper and simmer, lid askew, for 30 minutes.

Sprinkle the goulash with finely chopped parsley. Serve with boiled potatoes.

Preparation time: 30 minutes   Yield: 4 servings
Cooking time: 30 minutes

Braised Potatoes
Patátes Yiahní

SLICED POTATOES are cooked in tomatoes, onions and olive oil until permeated with the savory sauce and meltingly tender.

Serve this with salad, bread and some olives, or perhaps some fish roe spread, and you have a hearty winter meal.

> **2 pounds potatoes**
> **3 medium onions**
> **3/4 cup olive oil**
> **2 fresh ripe tomatoes,**
>   ***or* 1 (14 ounce) can tomatoes**
> **2 cups water**

1. Peel and quarter the potatoes.

2. *If using fresh tomatoes:* Halve them and grate them, cut side of the tomato against the coarse holes of the grater, until you are left holding only the skin.

If using canned tomatoes: Purée them in a food processor or put them through a vegetable mill.

3. Finely chop the onions. Sauté them in the oil until they wilt, add the tomatoes and season generously with salt and pepper. Simmer this sauce for five minutes.

4. Add the potatoes and the water, cover the pot and continue to simmer gently until the potatoes are tender and the sauce is not at all watery (about 45 minutes).

Preparation time: 20 minutes
Cooking time: 45 minutes

Yield: 4 servings

Layered Vegetable Bake
Briám

2 pounds potatoes
1 pound zucchini
4 onions
1/2 pound okra, fresh or frozen (may be omitted if not available)
3–4 cloves of garlic, sliced
3–4 tablespoons finely chopped parsley
3–4 tablespoons finely chopped dill
1 cup olive oil
1 cup tomatoes, pureed (about one 14 ounce can)
2 tomatoes, sliced
1/2 cup dry breadcrumbs

1. Peel the potatoes and slice them into rounds about 1/4-inch thick. Peel and slice the zucchini. Peel and slice 3 of the onions.

2. *If using fresh okra:* Wash it and trim the cone-shaped tops.

If using frozen okra: Use from frozen.

3. Make a single layer of potatoes in a deep baking dish, add a layer of zucchini, onions, a few garlic slices and a handful of okra. Season generously with salt and pepper and sprinkle with parsley and dill. Repeat these layers three or four more times, adding salt, pepper, parsley and dill with each layer. Add a final layer of potatoes.

4. Preheat the oven to 350°F.

5. Grate the remaining onion, or chop it very finely in a food processor. Sauté it in the oil until softened, then add the pureed tomatoes and 1/2 cup of water. Season with salt and pepper and simmer gently for 10 minutes.

6. Pour this sauce over the vegetable layers.

7. Cover the dish with the tomato slices and sprinkle with the dry breadcrumbs. Bake, uncovered, for 2 hours, or until a knife inserted into the centre of the dish encounters no resistance.

Preparation time: 1 hour   Yield: 5–6 servings
Baking time: 2 hours

Mushroom Stew
Manitária Kokkinistá

2 pounds mushrooms
2 large onions
5 ripe tomatoes *or* **1 large (28 ounce) can plum tomatoes**
3/4 cup olive oil
3 tablespoons ketchup
1 1/2 teaspoons oregano
1/4 cup finely chopped parsley

1. *If using fresh tomatoes:* Skin, seed and chop them.

If using canned tomatoes: Drain and chop them.

2. Peel the onions and grate them, or, alternatively, peel and quarter them and chop them very finely in a food processor.

3. Wash the mushrooms and cut them into bite-sized pieces.

4. Heat the oil and cook the onion on low heat for about 10 minutes. Add the tomatoes, mushrooms, ketchup and oregano. Season with salt and pepper and add one cup of water.

5. Adjust the heat and simmer, lid askew, for 45 minutes – 1 hour, or until the mushrooms are tender and the sauce is thick. Stir occasionally.

Adjust the seasoning and serve sprinkled with parsley and accompanied by rice.

Preparation time: 45 minutes   Yield: 4 servings
Cooking time: 1 hour

Potatoes Baked with Tahini Cream Sauce
Patátes Mousakás

2 pounds potatoes
2 onions
4–5 cloves of garlic
4–5 bay leaves

Sauce:
5 tablespoons tahini
2 tablespoons lemon juice

1. Preheat the oven to 375°F.

2. Peel the potatoes and the onions and cut them into slices (1/4 inch thick). Peel and chop the garlic.

3. Place a layer of potatoes in the base of a small baking dish. Top with slices of onion, garlic and a bay leaf and sprinkle with salt and pepper. Repeat these layers (reserving sufficient potato slices to make the final layer), until all the ingredients are used up. Cover the dish with a final layer of potato slices.

4. Add a cup of water to the dish and bake it, covered with a lid or aluminium foil, for about 1 hour 15 minutes, or until a knife meets with no resistance when it is pushed into the centre of the dish. Remove the dish from the oven and increase the oven heat to 450°F.

5. Place the tahini in a small bowl and stir in the lemon juice. Slowly add 1/2 cup of tepid water, stirring. Season this sauce with salt and pour it over the potatoes.

6. Place the dish back in the oven and bake for 15 minutes more until the surface begins to brown.

Serve hot with a green salad as a light lunch, or as a side.

Preparation time: 40 minutes   Yield: serves 4.
Baking time: 1 hour 30 minutes

Lima Beans
Fasólia Yiahní

IN THIS RECIPE the humble lima bean is transformed by simmering in a rich, thick tomato sauce. This is a substantial dish, which requires only good bread and perhaps some olives, slices of cucumber and tomato to complete the meal. It may be prepared ahead of time and improves upon being reheated.

- **1 pound dried Lima beans**
- **1 cup olive oil**
- **4 onions, grated, or chopped very finely in a food processor**
- **4–5 ripe tomatoes, *or* 1 (14 ounce) can tomatoes, puréed**
- **2–3 cloves of garlic, sliced**
- **1/2 cup finely chopped parsley**

1. Sort and rinse the beans discarding any foreign particles, cover them with water, boil them for 2–3 minutes and drain.

2. Bring a large pot of water to a boil, turn off the heat, add the beans and leave them to soak, covered, for about one hour.

3. Now turn the heat on to medium, return them to a boil and simmer them until they are half-cooked. This will take about an hour, according to the size, type and age of your beans. Strain them over a bowl, reserving the cooking liquid.

4. *If using fresh tomatoes:* Rinse and cut them in half. Grate them, cut side first, on the coarse side of a four-sided grater. You will be left holding the empty skins, which may be discarded.

5. Heat the oil in a large pot and cook the onion gently for about 10 minutes; it should become soft but not brown. Add the tomatoes, garlic, parsley and 1–2 cups of the reserved cooking liquid. Season with salt (about 1 1/2 teaspoons) and freshly ground black pepper.

6. Bring this sauce to a boil, add the beans and simmer them (lid askew) on medium-low heat for about an hour, or until the beans are tender and the sauce is thick.

7. If the beans float to the surface, place a heatproof plate on them to ensure that they cook in the sauce. Add more of the reserved cooking liquid if the sauce becomes too thick before the beans are tender. Taste and adjust the seasoning.

Preparation time: 30 minutes

Cooking and standing time: 3 hours

Yield: 5–6 servings

Lemon-Scented Chickpeas
Revíthia Lemonáta

1 pound dried chickpeas
2–3 tablespoons baking soda
3 onions
2–3 sweet green peppers
3/4–1 cup olive oil (optional)
2 teaspoons salt
Juice of 2 lemons

1. Place the chickpeas in a bowl; add enough water to cover them by about 3 inches and add a pinch of salt. Leave them to soak for between 12 and 24 hours.

2. Drain and put them in a large pot with hot water to cover, add the baking soda and bring to a boil. Boil the chickpeas for 3–4 minutes and drain through a colander.

3. Rinse the chickpeas and put them back in the pot. Add warm water to cover and rub them lightly between your fingers to remove their skins. The skins will float in the water above the chickpeas. Carefully pour this water, with the skins, through the colander, leaving the chickpeas in the pot. Cover them with water again and repeat this process until most of the skins have been removed. Discard the skins.

4. Add 5 cups of water to the chickpeas in the pot and put them on the heat to boil.

5. Peel and grate the onions, or quarter them and chop them very finely in a food processor. Add them to the pot.

6. Core, seed and quarter the peppers and chop them finely in the food processor. Add them to the chickpeas with the oil (if using) and the salt.

7. Once the chickpeas boil turn the heat to medium-low and allow them to simmer, lid askew, until they are tender. This will take between 1 and 3 hours. Check them regularly and do not allow them to become mushy. The sauce should be creamy but still soupy, if it becomes too dry during cooking, add a little extra hot water. Taste and adjust the seasoning.

Sprinkle generously with lemon juice to serve.

Preparation time: 40 minutes
Cooking: time 1–3 hours

Yield: 4–6 servings

Purée of Yellow Split Peas
Fáva

SOOTHING and creamy, this is comfort food for cold winter days.

> **1 pound yellow split peas**
> **1 onion, peeled and quartered**
> **2 potatoes, peeled and quartered**
> **2 small or 1 large sweet pepper, chopped**
> **1/2–1 cup olive oil (optional)**
> **4–5 green onions, finely chopped**
> **1/4 cup finely chopped dill (or substitute 1–2 tablespoons dried oregano)**
> **1 lemon**

1. Pour the split peas onto one side of a clean serving tray, pass them across the tray looking for and discarding any small stones. Place them in a sieve and rinse them with plenty of cold water.

2. Put the peas in a large pot, add 6 cups of water and bring them to a boil. Skim the foam that rises to the surface. Add the onion, potatoes, peppers, 1/2 cup of the oil (the oil is optional) and 1 teaspoon of salt.

3. When the peas return to a boil, cover the pot and lower the heat. Simmer the mixture gently until the peas are very soft. This will take about 1-2 hours, depending on the age and quality of the peas. If the peas are not cooked until they are very soft, the resulting purée will be gritty.

4. A blender or vegetable mill may be used to purée the contents of the pot. However, if the peas are cooked very slowly until they are very soft, then beating them with a wooden spoon will be sufficient to produce a creamy puree. Taste and add salt as necessary.

5. Beat the remaining olive oil with the lemon juice. Serve the purée in bowls, with the oil and lemon (again, omit the oil if desired), finely chopped dill and green onions for each person to add to taste.

This may be served hot, or more traditionally, at room temperature, in which case the purée will become thick and set like custard.

Preparation time: 30 minutes
Cooking time: 1 hour

Yield: 4 servings

Stewed Lentils

Fakés

PULSES such as lentils, chickpeas and lima beans have been an important component of the Greek diet since ancient times. They are often eaten in winter when the long boiling doesn't make the kitchen unbearably hot and when their intense nutrition is especially appreciated.

1 pound lentils
1 onion
5–6 cloves of garlic
2 skinned and chopped tomatoes,
    or **1/2 of a (14 ounce) can of plum tomatoes, chopped (optional)**
1 cup olive oil (optional)
2 bay leaves
3 tablespoons vinegar
1 tablespoon oregano

1. Sort the lentils and discard any pieces of grit. Rinse and place them in a large pot with water to cover and boil them for several minutes. Drain.

2. Peel and grate the onion (or peel and chop it very finely in a food processor). Peel and roughly chop the garlic.

3. Bring 6 cups of water to the boil and add the lentils with all the ingredients, including the oil optional, if you are using it, but not the tomatoes. (The tomatoes, if used, should be added midway through the cooking time).

4. Cook at a steady simmer with the lid askew for about an hour, or until the lentils are tender. Add salt to taste once the lentils are fully cooked.

May be served with bread and olives.

Preparation time: 30 minutes   Yield: 6 servings
Cooking time: 1 hour

Stuffed Peppers and Tomatoes

Piperiés kai Tomátes Gemistés

2 1/2 pounds sweet green peppers (about 10 medium)
4 pounds tomatoes (about 8 large)
4 onions
1 eggplant
2 cups olive oil
2 cups long grain rice
3–4 cloves of garlic, crushed to a pulp
1/2 cup finely chopped parsley

1. *Prepare the peppers:* Wash them and use a paring knife held horizontally to cut around each pepper about 1/2 inch from the top. This will create a "lid" for the pepper. Do not remove the stalks. Use a teaspoon to scrape out the pepper seeds and ribs. As you work, place each lid back on its corresponding pepper, where it should form a snug fit.

2. *Prepare the tomatoes:* Wash six of the tomatoes and slice them in two horizontally about 1/2 inch below the stem. Keep the two pieces of each tomato together. Use a teaspoon to scoop out the flesh and seeds (which should be reserved) and put a pinch of sugar inside each hollow tomato.

3. *Prepare the filling:* Peel and grate the onions on the course holes of a four-sided grater, or quarter them and chop them very finely in a food processor.

4. Peel and grate the eggplant. This may also be accomplished with a food processor (cut it into suitably-sized pieces first).

5. Cook the onion and the eggplant, in 1 cup of the oil, for 10 minutes over medium-low heat.

6. Take 1 cup of the reserved tomato flesh, chop it finely and add it to the onion mixture.

7. Purée all that remains of the reserved tomato flesh and seeds in a food processor, then push it through a sieve to remove the seeds. (Alternatively, purée and seed it simultaneously by pushing it all through a strong metal sieve with the back of a wooden spoon). Add 1 cup of the resulting tomato juice to the onion mixture.

8. Add the rice, garlic and parsley to the onion mixture along with 1/2 cup of water and stir well. When it returns to the boil, remove it from the heat and season it with salt (2 teaspoons) and freshly ground black pepper.

9. Preheat the oven to 350°F.

10. *Stuff the peppers and tomatoes:* Spoon some of the filling into each of the prepared vegetables. Do this lightly, do not press the stuffing into the vegetables and do not over-fill them. Leave about 1/2 inch of space unfilled at the top of each vegetable.

Keep in mind that the rice in the stuffing must have room to expand as it cooks, the "lids" must remain in place in order for the rice to remain moist and become tender.

11. Replace the "lid" on each vegetable as you work and stand them in a large, 2–3 inch deep, flat-bottomed baking dish. A roasting or lasagne pan works well here.

12. Measure the remaining tomato juice, if you have less than 1 cup then add water or use another tomato to make up the difference.

13. Spoon 1 cup of tomato juice and the remaining cup of olive oil over the stuffed vegetables. Sprinkle them with salt and pepper and bake them for 2 hours.

Allow them to stand for about an hour prior to serving.

Preparation time: 1 hour   Yield: 18 stuffed vegetables
Cooking time: 2 hours

Note on using extra ingredients:
If you have extra rice mixture, transfer it to a small saucepan, add about an equal volume of water (use tomato juice in place of some of the water if you also have this left over), cover and cook over gentle heat for about 20 minutes.

Stuffed Calamari
Kalamarákia Gemistá

CALAMARI (squid) are most usually cleaned by the fishmonger, or purchased frozen and ready to cook. It is important to wash them and to ensure that the tubes have been thoroughly cleaned before they are stuffed. You may prepare this recipe with the tubes alone (as they are sometimes sold when frozen) or with a mixture of tubes and tentacles.

> **2 pounds calamari, fresh or frozen**
> **2 onions**
> **6 plus 3 tablespoons olive oil**
> **1/2 cup long grain rice**
> **2 tablespoons raisins**
> **2 tablespoons pine nuts**
> **2 plus 1 tablespoons finely chopped parsley**
> **1/2 cup dry white wine**
> **4 tablespoons puréed tomato**
> **Plain wooden toothpicks**

1. *If using frozen calamari:* Place them in a bowl of cold water and set them aside to defrost, changing the water once or twice.

If using fresh calamari: Proceed with step 2.

2. Peel the onions and grate them, or chop them very finely in a food processor. Heat 6 tablespoons of olive oil in a frying pan and add the onions. Cover and cook gently for 10 minutes, stirring occasionally.

3. Add the rice, raisins, pine nuts and 2 tablespoons of parsley. Season with a teaspoon of salt and a little ground black pepper. Stir this mixture well and remove it from the heat.

4. Check that the calamari tubes have been thoroughly cleaned and if necessary remove any remaining pieces of cartilage (the cartilage looks like long pieces of clear plastic and is not difficult to find and remove). Cut a tiny piece off the end of each tube to allow water to run through freely. Wash them, rub them with salt and rinse again. Drain them well. Any tentacles to be used in the recipe should also be rinsed in water.

5. Place about 2 teaspoons of the rice mixture into each calamari tube and secure the openings with toothpicks. Do not overstuff the calamari otherwise they may burst when they are cooked. Chop the tentacles along with any tubes for which there is insufficient rice stuffing.

6. Preheat the oven to 350°F.

7. Heat the remaining 4 tablespoons of oil in the frying pan and add the stuffed calamari, along with any chopped tentacles. Sauté for 2–3 minutes then pour the wine over them. Allow the wine to bubble for a couple of minutes then remove the calamari with a slotted spoon. Arrange the stuffed tubes of the calamari close together, but in a single layer, in a baking dish, and scatter any chopped tentacles in the dish too.

8. Add the puréed tomato and the remaining tablespoon of parsley to the wine in the frying pan and season lightly with salt and pepper. Cook the sauce for 3–4 minutes, stirring, until it blends. Pour this sauce over the calamari in the baking dish.

9. Bake the dish, uncovered, for 1 hour, until the rice is tender.

Preparation time: 1 hour 30 minutes   Yield: 4 servings
Baking time: 1 hour

Stuffed Eggplants

Melitzánes Papoutsákia

THE GREEK NAME for these means 'eggplant shoes', an apt description of the stuffed and baked eggplant halves. The ability of the eggplant to soak up olive oil is legendary and the partnership is a good one.

> **4 medium eggplants (about 2 pounds)**
> **1 cup plus 4 tablespoons olive oil**
> **2 onions**
> **3 cloves garlic**
> **4 ripe tomatoes, *or* 1 (14 ounce) can plum tomatoes**
> **3 thick slices day-old French or Italian bread (about 3 ounces)**
> **1/4 cup finely chopped parsley**
> **1/2 cup dry breadcrumbs**

1. Cut the eggplants in half lengthwise. Sprinkle the cut surfaces with salt and place them in a colander. Allow to stand for one hour.

2. Rinse the eggplants and wipe them dry. Use a sharp knife to make a deep incision in the shape of a cross in the cut surface of each eggplant half. Take care not to cut the skins.

3. Divide the cup of olive oil between two frying pans and heat it. Place the eggplant halves, cut side down, in the frying pans and cook them on medium-low heat for 10 minutes. They will absorb the oil as they cook. Set them aside to cool.

4. Peel and grate the onions, or chop them very finely in a food processor.

5. Peel the garlic and crush it to a pulp.

6. *If using fresh tomatoes:* Skin the tomatoes and purée them.

If using canned tomatoes: Purée the contents of the can in a food processor, or through a vegetable mill.

7. Remove the flesh from the eggplants, taking care not to tear the skins, and cut it into small dice. Arrange the empty skins in one large or two smaller baking dishes.

8. Remove the crust from the bread. (If it is moist and fresh, dry it in the oven for 10 minutes at 300°F.) Soak it in a little tepid water then press it between your palms to remove as much moisture as possible.

9. Preheat the oven to 350°F.

10. Heat the remaining 4 tablespoons of oil in a frying pan on medium heat. Add the onion and cook for 5 minutes, stirring.

11. Add the eggplant dice and tomato purée to the onions and continue to cook for 5–10 minutes or until the eggplant is tender. Add the garlic, cook for one minute.

12. Crumble the bread into the eggplant mixture; add the parsley and season to taste with salt and pepper. Stir well and remove from the heat.

13. Heap this mixture into the eggplant skins. Sprinkle with the dry breadcrumbs and bake for 30 minutes.

Preparation time: 40 minutes   Yield: 4 servings
Baking time: 30 minutes

Stuffed Vine Leaves
Dolmadákia me Ambelófylla

1 pound preserved or fresh grape vine leaves
1 1/2 cups long grain rice
1 medium onion
8–9 green onions
2 tablespoons finely chopped dill
2 tablespoons finely chopped parsley
1/4 cup pine nuts
1/2 cup olive oil
Juice of 1–2 lemons

1. *If using preserved vine leaves:* Place them in a large pot of boiling water and cook for 4–5 minutes (this will increase their tenderness). Drain.

If using fresh vine leaves: they should be washed and blanched briefly, a handful at a time, in boiling water.

2. *To prepare the filling:* Peel and grate the onion (or chop it very finely in a food processor). Wash and finely chop the green onions. Combine these with the rice and add the dill, parsley, pine nuts, salt (about 1 1/4 teaspoons) and pepper and 1/4 cup of the oil.

3. *To stuff the vine leaves:* Place a vine leaf, shiny side down on your work surface and put 1 teaspoon of filling in the centre of the leaf. Fold the leaf over the filling, tuck in the edges and roll it up to completely enclose the filling in a little oblong packet. Give the stuffed leaf a gentle squeeze in the palm of one hand and set it aside. Continue in this way until all the leaves are stuffed, reserve any damaged or extra-large leaves.

4. Line the base of a cooking pot with the damaged or extra large leaves, and arrange the stuffed leaves on these side by side and in layers.

5. Add the remaining oil and the lemon juice to the pot. Place a heatproof plate on the stuffed leaves and carefully pour in two cups of boiling water. Cover and simmer until the water is absorbed and only the oil remains (about 45 minutes). Check the rice for tenderness, if it is necessary to extend the cooking time then add a little extra hot water.

Preparation time: 1 hour
Cooking time: 45 minutes

Yield: 4 servings

Stuffed Zucchini
Kolokythákia Gemistá

Hollow logs of zucchini stuffed with savory rice. As with most stuffed vegetable dishes, they require longer than average preparation time and are best prepared on weekends spent around the house. They are not at all difficult to make well and the extra effort is rewarded by the resulting dish which transforms the humble zucchini into a special meal.

> 10–12 long, plump zucchini
> Juice of 1 lemon
> 2 medium onions
> 4 green onions
> 1 medium eggplant
> 2 cloves of garlic
> 1 cup olive oil
> 1/2 cup finely chopped parsley
> 1 (6 ounce) can tomato paste
> 1 1/2 cups medium grain rice
> 3 tablespoons flour
> 4 tablespoons margarine

1. Peel the zucchini and plunge them into boiling salted water. When the water returns to the boil strain them through a colander.

2. When they are cool enough to handle, cut them into 2-inch lengths. Using a small teaspoon, or a potato peeler, remove part of the flesh and the seeds from the centre of each length of zucchini taking care not to break them. The zucchini should now resemble little hollow logs.

3. Arrange the zucchini in an oiled baking dish and sprinkle them with a little lemon juice.

4. Peel and halve the onions and grate them on the coarse side of a four-sided grater. Alternatively, quarter them and chop them very finely in a food processor. Finely chop the green onions. Peel and grate the eggplant. Peel the garlic and crush it to a pulp.

5. Heat 1/2 cup of the oil in a saucepan and sauté both kinds of onions, the eggplant and garlic. Add a cup of water, the parsley, tomato paste and rice and season with salt and pepper. Stir the mixture well and remove it from the heat.

6. Preheat the oven to 400°F.

7. Stuff the zucchini logs with the rice mixture and sprinkle them with the remaining 1/2 cup of oil and with 1 cup of water. Cover the dish with aluminium foil, in which make 2–3 holes to allow the steam to escape.

8. Bake them until the rice is tender, this will take between 1 hour and 1 hour 30 minutes. If they are becoming dry during cooking, add a little additional hot water with some lemon juice.

9. Once they are ready, remove them to a serving dish and pour the cooking liquid into a measuring jug adding sufficient water to make a total of 2 1/2 cups of liquid.

10. Melt the margarine in a saucepan and add the flour. Cook this, stirring, for 1–2 minutes. Add the cooking liquid and season with salt, pepper and lemon juice to taste. Stir the sauce until it simmers and thickens and pour it over the zucchini.

Preparation time 1 hour   Yield 6 servings
Cooking time 1 hour – 1 hour 30 minutes

DESSERTS

SECTION THREE

Oranges in Syrup with Candied Peel

Portokália me Glykó apo ti Flouda tous

6 Navel (thick-skinned) oranges
1 1/2 cups sugar
Juice of 1/2 lemon
1 tablespoon orange liquor or brandy

1. Scrub two of the oranges well and use a sharp paring knife to score the peel vertically into quarters. Pull the peel away from the oranges and reserve. Trim the oranges of any remaining white pith.

2. Cut the reserved peel into thin 1/2-inch lengths. Place it in a saucepan with 4–5 cups of water and bring to a boil. Boil for 30 minutes and drain.

3. Wash the remaining oranges and use a paring knife to peel them, cutting deeply enough to remove the white pith. Slice all six oranges horizontally into thick discs, putting each orange back together as you work. Place each orange in an individual serving dish; or arrange them together in a large serving bowl.

4. Put the boiled and drained peel back in the saucepan with the sugar and three tablespoons of water. Bring it slowly to a boil then simmer for 5 minutes.

5. Remove the saucepan from the heat and stir in the lemon juice and orange liquor or brandy.

6. Spoon some of the syrup with the candied peel over each orange. Any extra syrup and candied peel may be stored in the refrigerator and used for another purpose.

Refrigerate the oranges and serve them chilled.

Preparation time: 50 minutes
Refrigeration time: 2 hours

Yield: 6 servings

Apple Tart
Tárta me Míla

Base:
2 cups flour
1 teaspoon baking powder
1 tablespoon sugar
1 stick margarine (4 ounces), cold
4–5 tablespoons water or brandy

Filling:
3 tablespoons apricot jam
4 apples
1/2 cup sugar
1/3 cup coarsely chopped walnuts
Ground cinnamon

Topping:
2 tablespoons honey
1/2 cup golden raisins
2 tablespoons margarine
1 cup coarsely ground walnuts

1. *Prepare the pastry base:* Mix the flour, sugar and baking powder. Add the margarine and rub the mixture between the fingers until it becomes crumbly. Sprinkle it with the water and gather it into a ball.

2. Divide the dough into two pieces, wrap one piece in cling wrap and set it aside. Roll out the other piece and use it to line a 9-inch pie dish. Warm the apricot jam and brush it over the dough in the dish.

3. Preheat the oven to 400°F.

4. *Prepare the filling:* Peel, core and thinly slice the apples, toss them gently in the sugar, a little ground cinnamon and the walnuts. Arrange the apple slices on the pastry base and bake it for 15 minutes.

5. *Prepare the topping:* Heat the honey, raisins and margarine gently until melted and stir in the ground walnuts. Spread this mixture over the apple filling. Roll out the remaining dough and cut it into strips. Arrange the pastry strips in a lattice over the tart and bake for 30 minutes.

Preparation time: 1 hour   Yield: one 9-inch tart
Baking time: 45 minutes

Apple Cake
Kéïk me Mila

THIS FAST, simple recipe produces a moist cake which is even better if wrapped in aluminum foil and kept until the following day.

- 2/3 **cup corn oil**
- 1 1/3 **cups sugar**
- 2 **large Granny Smith apples**
- 2 **cups self-rising flour**
- 1/2 **teaspoon baking soda**
- 1 **tablespoon ground cinnamon**
- 1/2 **cup ground walnuts**

1. Preheat the oven to 350°F and oil a 9-inch springform pan.

2. Beat the oil with the sugar.

3. Peel and grate the apples and stir them into the sugar mixture.

4. Add the dry ingredients and mix well. You should have a thick batter. If it seems too dry, add a little water or orange juice.

5. Spoon the batter into the pan and bake for 1 hour.

Preparation time: 30 minutes
Baking time: 1 hour

Yield: one 9-inch cake

Date and Walnut Cake
Kéïk me Hourmádes

1 1/2 cups chopped dates (about 8 ounces)
1 cup boiling water
1 tablespoon margarine
1 cup sugar
2 teaspoons vanilla essence
1 1/2 cups all-purpose flour
1 teaspoon baking soda
21/2 tablespoons brandy
1/2 cup finely chopped walnuts

Glaze:
1/2 cup sugar
1/2 cup finely chopped dates (2–3 ounces)
1/4 cup water
1/2 cup finely chopped walnuts

1. Preheat the oven to 350°F and grease a 9-inch springform pan.

2. *Prepare the cake:* Combine the boiling water with the dates and margarine in a mixing bowl.

3. Add the sugar, vanilla and flour. Dissolve the baking soda in the brandy and add this to the mixture. Beat for 2 minutes.

4. Stir in the walnuts.

5. Pour the cake batter into the prepared pan and bake for 30 minutes.

6. Cool the cake for 10–15 minutes before removing it from the pan. Allow the cake to cool completely.

7. *Prepare the glaze:* Combine the sugar, dates and water in a small saucepan and simmer, stirring, for 2 minutes. Add the walnuts, stir, and pour the mixture over the cake. Allow to cool.

Preparation time: 30 minutes
Baking time: 30 minutes

Yield: one 9-inch cake

Baklava
Baklavás

COMMERCIAL phyllo dough must be defrosted before use. Keep it wrapped until you are ready to begin constructing the baklava, if it is exposed to air it will become dry and difficult to use. Neatness is not advantageous here – the resulting pie is made lighter by allowing the sheets of phyllo to make little pleats and folds in the pan, and by occasional sprinkles of water between the layers as they are constructed.

Pie:
1 pound phyllo dough, defrosted
1/2 pound margarine or 1 cup vegetable oil
14 ounces shelled walnuts
1 tablespoon cinnamon

Syrup:
3 1/2 cups sugar
1/2 cup light corn syrup
2 cups water

1. *Prepare the filling:* Coarsely grind the walnuts and combine them with the cinnamon.

2. *Construct the pie:* Melt the margarine, or put the oil into a small bowl. Brush a 13 by 9 by 2-inch baking pan (or similar three quart capacity baking dish) with a little oil or margarine.

3. Preheat the oven to 400°F.

4. Open the phyllo dough and brush the first sheet in the stack with the oil or margarine. Lay it in the baking pan; do not try to stretch it out but allow it to form little creases and pleats. Repeat with 7 more sheets of dough, filling the pan evenly.

5. Wrap and set aside 8 sheets of phyllo dough, these will be used for the last layers of the baklava.

6. Sprinkle 2 tablespoons of the walnut mixture into the pan. Brush another sheet of phyllo dough with oil or margarine and lay it over the walnut filling allowing it to form creases and pleats as before.

7. Continue to alternate filling and phyllo dough until no more filling remains, sprinkling some of the layers with half a teaspoon or so of water as you work. Brush the reserved sheets of dough with oil and lay them in the pan.

8. Use a sharp knife to cut through the top layers of the pie, first making 4 cuts horizontally across the

length of the pan then making 7 cuts diagonally across the width of the pan. This will make about 26 diamond-shaped pieces of baklava.

9. Bake the baklava for 15 minutes then reduce the oven temperature to 350°F and bake the baklava for about 45 minutes, until golden.

10. *Prepare the syrup:* As the pie cools; heat the ingredients for the syrup slowly, stirring, until the sugar dissolves. Then allow the mixture to simmer for 5–6 minutes.

11. Pour the syrup over the baklava and allow it to stand until it is completely cooled and the syrup has been absorbed.

Preparation time: 1 hour   Yield: about 26 pieces
Baking time: 1 hour

Butter Cream Sandwiches

Kéïk Yemistó me Kréma

THIS UNUSUAL sweet bread is delicious with tea or coffee. It is baked in a rectangular cake pan and cut into squares, which are made into sandwiches with a butter cream filling and a sweet and crunchy almond topping.

Sweet Dough:
1 cup warm water
Pinch of sugar
1 envelope dried yeast
4 cups self-rising flour
1/4 cup sugar
4 tablespoons margarine
3 tablespoons brandy
1/2 teaspoon grated lemon zest

Topping:
3 tablespoons margarine
3/4 cup sugar
5 ounces raw almonds, finely chopped (about 1 cup)
1 tablespoon cold water

Filling:
6 tablespoons margarine, at room temperature
1 cup powdered sugar
1 teaspoon vanilla essence

1. Line a 13-inch by 9-inch rectangular baking pan with parchment paper and coat it lightly with margarine.

1. *Prepare the dough:* Dissolve the yeast in the warm water with a pinch of sugar. Leave it in a warm place for 5–10 minutes until bubbles appear on the surface.

2. Combine the sugar with the flour in a mixing bowl.

3. Melt the 4 tablespoons of margarine in a small bowl; allow it to cool slightly and add the yeast mixture, brandy and lemon peel, stirring well.

4. Pour the margarine mixture into the bowl with the flour and sugar and mix and knead the ingredients until you have a soft dough.

5. Place the dough in the pan and press it into the corners of the prepared baking pan with your fingers. Do not worry if it seems too flat since the dough will rise significantly as it rests, and again in the oven.

5. Cover it and leave it to rise in a warm place for 1–1 1/2 hours.

6. Preheat oven to 400°F.

7. *Prepare the topping:* Melt the 3 tablespoons of margarine, add the 3/4 cup of sugar, almonds and cold water. Sprinkle this mixture over the risen dough.

8. Bake for 40 minutes.

9. Cut the cake into squares (about 2 1/2 inch by 2 1/2 inch) when it is still slightly warm. Allow the pieces to cool completely.

10. *For the butter cream filling:* Beat the margarine with the powdered sugar and the vanilla.

11. Slice a square of cake horizontally, spread a little of the filling on one of the cut sides and sandwich the two pieces back together. Repeat with the remaining pieces of cake.

Preparation time 40 minutes   Yield 15 pieces
Rising time 1–1 1/2 hours
Baking time 40 minutes

Biscotti
Paximádia

MASTIC GUM gives these twice-baked treats a special flavor. It is produced from the gum of the mastic trees of the island of Chios and may be found at Greek food stores, or mail-ordered. The little rocks are pounded immediately prior to use; if you don't have a pestle and mortar, place the rocks in a small bowl and crush them with the end of the handle of a wooden spoon. A pinch of sugar will prevent it from adhering to your kitchen equipment, and will help to grind it to a fine powder.

If mastic gum is not available, it may be omitted; the resulting biscotti will be different but still delicious.

    1 cup corn oil
    1 1/2 cups sugar
    1 cup orange juice
    Juice of 1 lemon
    1 teaspoon baking soda
    3–4 rocks mastic gum, pounded (about 1 teaspoon)
    1 tablespoon ground cinnamon
    6 cups all-purpose flour

1. Preheat the oven to 375°F.

2. Beat the oil with the sugar and add the orange juice.

3. Dissolve the baking soda in the lemon juice and add this to the oil mixture.

4. Add the flour, cinnamon and mastic gum, stirring and kneading until you have a soft dough.

5. Divide the dough into two and, on a baking tray, shape each half into a rectangle, about 12 inches long by 4 inches wide and 3/4 inch thick. Score these into 3/4 inch-wide fingers.

6. Bake them for 40 minutes, until golden.

7. Remove them from the oven and reduce the oven temperature to 300°F. Cut the fingers on the score lines with a sharp knife, separate them and place them cut side down on the baking tray. Return them to the oven for 15 minutes. Turn them over and bake them for a further 15 minutes. Allow to cool before storing.

Preparation time: 20 minutes   Yield: 30 pieces
Baking time: 1 hour 10 minutes

Chocolate Cake
Kéïk me Kakáo

1 cup plus 2 tablespoons margarine, at room temperature
1 1/3 cups sugar
1/3 cup orange juice
1/3 cup cocoa powder
2 teaspoons coffee extract *or* instant coffee powder dissolved in 2 teaspoons water
2 cups plus 2 tablespoons self-raising flour
6 tablespoons water
4 ounces (about 1/2 cup) maraschino cherries
3 1/2 ounces (about 1 cup) coarsely ground walnuts

Glaze:
1 1/4 cups powdered sugar
3 tablespoons cocoa powder
4–5 tablespoons brandy
1 tablespoon margarine
Coarsely ground walnuts to decorate

1. Preheat the oven to 350°F. Grease and line a 9-inch springform pan.

2. Beat the margarine until it is light, continue to beat and add, gradually, the sugar and the orange juice. Stir in the cocoa, coffee extract, flour and water.

3. Rinse the cherries, halve and pit them if necessary, and toss them in flour to coat. Add the cherries and the walnuts into the batter. Stir to combine.

4. Spoon the batter into the prepared pan, spreading it evenly and bake it for 50 minutes, or until a skewer inserted into the centre comes out clean.

5. Allow the cake to cool for 10 minutes, then remove the side of the pan, invert the cake onto a plate and remove the base of the pan and the lining.

6. *Make the glaze:* Combine the sugar, cocoa and brandy in a small bowl. Melt the margarine and add it to the glaze. Spread this over the cake and sprinkle it with the walnuts.

Preparation time: 30 minutes   Yield: 10–12 servings
Baking time: 50 minutes

Chocolate Log
Kormós Kariókas

8 ounces (2 cups) shelled walnuts, coarsely chopped
5 ounces (1/3 of a box) Graham crackers
1/2 cup sugar
1 cup water
2 tablespoons margarine
5 ounces dark chocolate, in small pieces

Chocolate coating:
5 ounces dark chocolate, in small pieces
3 ounces (3/4 cup) shelled walnuts, coarsely chopped

1. *Prepare the filling:* Crush the Graham crackers.

2. Put these in a saucepan with the walnuts, sugar, water, margarine and chocolate. Heat gently and allow to simmer for 5 minutes, stirring to prevent burning and sticking, until you have a thick mass that pulls away from the sides of the pan. Put this in the refrigerator to cool.

3. Preheat the oven to 350°F.

4. *Prepare the chocolate coating:* Put the walnuts on a baking tray and toast them in the oven for 10 minutes, stirring once or twice.

5. Bring about an inch of water to the boil in a small saucepan. Remove it from the heat and set a small bowl over the pan. Put the chocolate in the bowl and stir until it melts.

6. Stir the walnuts into the melted chocolate.

7. *Construct the log:* Spread a piece of aluminum foil, about 18 inches long, on a work surface. Put the cooled filling mixture on the foil and shape it into a cylinder, about 12 inches long, 5 inches in diameter. Carefully spread the melted chocolate mixture over the log and wrap it loosely in the foil.

8. Refrigerate the log until firm, about 3 hours.

Store in the refrigerator. Slice to serve.

Preparation time: 1 hour
Refrigeration time: 3 hours

Yield: 12 servings

Chocolate Treats
Sokolatákia me Karydia

**10 ounces (2 1/2 cups) shelled walnuts
10 ounces dark chocolate**

1. Preheat the oven to 350°F.

2. Spread the walnuts on a dry baking tray and toast them in the oven for 10 minutes, stirring once or twice.

3. Put the walnuts on a chopping board and chop them into roughly pea-sized pieces.

4. *Melt the chocolate:* Fill a small saucepan with water to a depth of about 1 inch and bring it to a boil. When it boils, remove it from the heat and set a small bowl on the pan. Place the chocolate in the bowl and stir until melted and smooth.

5. Combine the walnuts with the melted chocolate and stir until the nuts are well coated.

6. Line a baking tray with greaseproof kitchen paper or mini baking cups and, using two teaspoons, place bite-sized heaps of the nut mixture onto the paper or into the cups.

7. Place the tray into the refrigerator for about an hour, until set.

Store the treats in the refrigerator.

Preparation time: 40 minutes
Refrigeration time: 1 hour

Yield: about 40 pieces

Other variations:

Try replacing the walnuts with 2 cups of almonds or hazelnuts. Follow the recipe above, but do not chop the nuts.

Honeyed Spice Cookies
Finíkia

1 cup vegetable oil
1/2 cup olive oil
1/2 cup sugar
1/2 cup orange juice
1 teaspoon baking soda
1 tablespoon ground cinnamon
1 teaspoon grated lemon zest
4 cups all purpose flour

Syrup and Topping:
1 1/2 cups sugar
1 cup water
1 tablespoon honey
1/2 cup finely chopped walnuts

1. Preheat the oven to 350°F.

2. Combine the corn oil, olive oil and sugar in a mixing bowl.

3. Dissolve the soda in the orange juice and add it to the oil and sugar mixture.

4. Add the cinnamon, lemon zest and flour and mix until you have a soft dough.

5. Pinch off portions of the dough and roll them into little cylinders, about an inch wide and 2 inches long. Press them to flatten them slightly with the palm of your hand. Arrange them on two baking trays and bake them for about 20 minutes, until no longer doughy.

6. *Prepare the syrup:* Place the sugar, water and honey in a small pan and heat it gently, stirring occasionally, until the sugar dissolves. Adjust the heat so that the syrup simmers steadily and cook for 5 minutes. Remove it from the heat.

7. Place the cookies in the syrup, half a dozen at a time. Turn them carefully allowing each batch to remain in the syrup for about 30 seconds. Remove them to a serving tray with a slotted spoon and sprinkle them immediately with the chopped walnuts.

Preparation time: 40 minutes   Yield: about 40 cookies
Baking time: 20 minutes

Cream of Wheat Dessert
Halvás Simigdalénios

4 cups water
2 cups sugar
1 cup margarine or corn oil
2 cups cream of wheat
1 teaspoon almond essence
1 cup blanched almonds, or pine nuts

1. Place the water and sugar over medium heat, stirring occasionally, until the sugar dissolves. Turn the heat to medium-high and boil the syrup for 5 minutes. Set aside.

2. Toast the almonds in a dry frying pan over medium heat for 3–4 minutes, stirring. Do not allow them to burn.

3. Heat the oil in a large, deep pot and add the cream of wheat. Stir over medium heat until the cream of wheat is pale golden.

4. Carefully pour the syrup into the cream of wheat, add the almond essence, and nuts. Cook, stirring, until the mixture becomes thick and pulls away from the sides of the pot.

5. Remove from the heat and allow to stand, covered with a kitchen towel, for 30 minutes.

6. Put the mixture into a 2-quart bundt pan or similar decorative mould. When it is cool turn it out and sprinkle it with ground cinnamon. It might also be placed in, and served directly from, a rectangular dish.

Preparation time: 30 minutes   Yield: 8 servings
Standing and cooling time: 2 hours

Mandarin Torte
Toúrta Mandaríni

Base:
1 1/2 cups self-rising flour
1/4 teaspoon salt
1/4 cup olive or vegetable oil
Juice and finely grated zest of 1 mandarin
1/2 cup sugar
1 cup water

Cream:
3 1/2 pounds mandarins (clementines, satsumas or tangerines)
1 cup water
1/2 cup cornstarch
3/4 cup sugar

Decoration:
1/2 cup finely chopped or slivered almonds

1. Preheat the oven to 350°F.

2. Grease a 9-inch springform pan and line the base with parchment paper.

3. *To prepare the base:* Combine the flour and the salt in a mixing bowl. Add the oil, mandarin juice and zest, sugar and water. Mix well, without beating.

4. Pour the batter into the prepared baking pan and bake it for 45–50 minutes, until the cake pulls away from the sides of the pan.

5. Let the cake rest for about 10 minutes, then remove it from the pan and invert it onto a cooling rack. Remove the parchment paper.

6. Brush any excess crumbs from the cake pan and set it aside for use when assembling the torte.

7. *To prepare the cream:* Set aside one of the mandarins and juice the rest. Measure 2 1/2 cups of the juice and pour it, through a sieve, into a saucepan. Add one cup of water and bring it to a boil.

8. Dilute the cornstarch in 6 tablespoons of cold water. Add it to the hot mandarin juice, stirring. Continue to stir and heat the mixture gently until it simmers and thickens, about 5 minutes. Remove it from the heat and stir in the sugar.

9. Place the cake, still inverted, back into the springform pan and sprinkle it with the juice and finely grated zest of the reserved mandarin. Pour the mandarin cream onto this base (if the cream is not perfectly smooth, press it through a sieve). Place it in the refrigerator to cool and set (2–3 hours).

10. Place the almonds in a dry frying pan and toast them, stirring, for 2–3 minutes over medium high heat. Do not let them burn.

11. Carefully remove the sides of the springform pan and serve the torte sprinkled with the toasted almonds.

Preparation time: 1 hour   Yield 8 servings: (one 9-inch torte)
Baking time: 50 minutes
Refrigeration: 2–3 hours

Coconut Shortbread Cookies
Kourambiédes me Indokárydo

8 ounces margarine, at room temperature
4 tablespoons sugar
2 cups coconut flakes
2 cups all-purpose flour
1 cup powdered sugar

1. Preheat the oven to 350°F.

2. Beat the margarine until it is smooth and light.

3. Add the 4 tablespoons of sugar, the coconut flakes and flour, mix them and bring them together into a ball.

4. Take tablespoon-sized pieces of the dough and roll them into little balls, flatten them very slightly between the palms of your hands and place them on baking trays.

5. Bake them for 20 minutes. They should still be pale; over-baking will cause them to fall apart.

6. Sift a generous layer of powdered sugar over them when they are still warm. (You could also add a little more sugar immediately before serving.)

Preparation time: 15 minutes   Yield: 40 cookies
Baking time: 20 minutes

European-Style Cookies
Koulourákia

THESE STORE well if they are kept in a cool, dry place, such as a cake or cookie tin. They are everyday cookies to serve with tea or coffee. The sesame seeds give them a nice nutty flavor.

1 cup olive or vegetable oil
1 cup sugar
1 teaspoon baking soda
2 tablespoons brandy
Juice of 1 orange (about 1/4 cup)
3 1/2 cups all-purpose flour
1/2 cup sesame seeds

1. Preheat the oven to 375°F

2. Beat the oil with the sugar in a mixing bowl.

3. Dissolve the baking soda in the brandy (it will fizz), and add it, together with the orange juice, to the oil mixture.

4. Add the flour, stir and gather the mixture into a soft ball of dough.

5. Take walnut-size pieces of dough and roll them in your hands then flatten them slightly to produce little oblongs. Place them on a baking tray and sprinkle them with sesame seeds.

6. Bake the cookies for 15 minutes, until golden.

Cool on a rack.

Preparation time: 20 minutes   Yield: about 40 cookies
Baking time: 15 minutes

Hazelnut Shortbread Cookies
Kourambiédes me Foundoúkia

LITTLE SHORTBREAD cookies are made for special occasions in Greece. They are sometimes wrapped decoratively to be given as wedding favors. They store well and make pleasant treats for any occasion.

3 1/2 cups shelled hazelnuts
2 1/2 cups flour
1 cup plus 2 tablespoons margarine, at room temperature
4 tablespoons sugar
1–2 cups powdered sugar

1. Preheat the oven to 350°F.

2. Place 2 1/2 cups of the hazelnuts on a baking tray and toast them in the oven for 6–7 minutes.

3. When the hazelnuts are sufficiently cool, grind them finely in a food processor.

4. Beat the margarine until it is light, add the flour, the 4 tablespoons of sugar and the ground hazelnuts. Mix the ingredients and gather them up into a ball.

5. Preheat the oven to 375°F.

6. Take tablespoon-sized pieces of dough, shape them into mounds and place them on a baking tray.

7. Press a whole hazelnut into each mound and bake for 20 minutes. These should not brown; do not be tempted to bake them for longer than the time given because over-cooking will cause them to fall apart.

8. Allow them to cool on the baking tray for 10 minutes or so then sprinkle them with a generous amount of powdered sugar by shaking it through a sieve over the tray.

Preparation time: 45 minutes   Yield: 50 small cookies
Baking time: 20 minutes

Lemon Shortbread Cookies
Koulourákia

THIS DOUGH also works well in a cookie press if it is first thinned with a little soymilk. The cookies will keep well if stored in an airtight container, perfect to serve on the arrival of unexpected guests.

2 sticks margarine, at room temperature
1 cup powdered sugar
2 cups all-purpose flour
Finely grated zest of 1/2 lemon (or substitute 1 teaspoon vanilla essence)
3 tablespoons soymilk (for cookie press only)

1. Preheat the oven to 400°F.

2. Beat the margarine with the sugar. Add the flour and the lemon zest, or vanilla essence, and mix well.

3. *To shape cookies by hand:* Take small, walnut-sized pieces of dough and roll them into balls between the palms of your hands. Press them lightly between the palms to make little discs and place on an un-greased cookie sheet.

4. *To use this dough in a cookie press:* Thin the dough with about 3 tablespoons of soymilk and use to fill cookie press according to manufacturer's directions. Press the cookies onto an un-greased baking sheet.

5. Bake for 6–12 minutes (the hand-shaped kind will take longer to bake), until pale golden around the edges.

Preparation time: 30 minutes   Yield: about 3 dozen small cookies

Shredded Pastry and Walnut Fingers
Kataifi

1 pound kataifi dough, defrosted
14 ounces shelled walnuts
1 tablespoon ground cinnamon
1/2 teaspoon ground clove
3 1/4 sticks (13 ounces) margarine

Syrup:
5 cups sugar
3 1/2 cups water
1 tablespoon lemon juice

1. Coarsely grind the walnuts and add the cinnamon and clove.

2. Preheat the oven to 350°F.

3. Pull the kataifi dough apart, using your fingers to separate the strands. Let them fall lightly into a heap on your work surface.

4. Take a half cup of kataifi, place it on your work surface and tease it into a rectangle roughly 3x5 inches. Put 2 tablespoons of the walnut filling along the short end of the rectangle and, beginning at this end, roll it up to enclose the filling in a little cylinder. Repeat this with the remaining dough and filling. Place the rolls on greased baking pans or sheets, leaving about an inch between them to allow even baking.

5. Melt the margarine and drizzle one tablespoon of margarine over each roll. Bake for 30 minutes, until pale golden.

6. *Prepare the syrup as the rolls cool:* Put the water, sugar and lemon juice into a large saucepan. Heat gently and stir until the sugar dissolves. Adjust the heat to produce a steady simmer and cook for 5 minutes.

7. If your baking pan does not have raised sides, transfer the rolls to another container, arranging them close together. If you used two baking pans, transfer them all onto one with raised sides, thus they will better absorb the syrup. Ladle the syrup over the kataifi rolls and let stand for 8 hours or overnight.

Preparation time: 1 hour 30 minutes   Yield: 25–30 pieces
Baking time: 30 minutes
Standing time: 8 hours

Nut Roll

Roló me Karydia

Dough:
1 stick (4 ounces) margarine, at room temperature
1/2 cup sugar
Grated zest of 1/2 lemon
1 tablespoon lemon juice
2 1/2 tablespoons brandy
2 1/2 cups flour
1 teaspoon baking powder

Filling:
4 tablespoons water
1 tablespoon honey
1/2 cup sugar
2 teaspoons cornstarch
2 1/2 cups ground walnuts
1 teaspoon cinnamon
1/2 cup golden raisins
Powdered sugar

1. *To prepare the dough:* Beat the margarine until it is soft and light. Continue to beat, gradually incorporating the sugar, lemon zest, lemon juice and brandy.

2. Sieve the flour with the baking powder and add it to the margarine mixture. Mix, then knead, until you have a smooth ball of dough. Wrap the dough in cling wrap, or put it in a zip lock bag, and chill.

3. *To prepare the filling:* Heat the honey and the sugar in the water until they dissolve. Dissolve the cornstarch in 1 tablespoon of cold water and add to the syrup, stirring. Cook gently for one more minute, remove from the heat and stir in the walnuts, cinnamon and raisins.

4. Preheat the oven to 350°F.

5. *To assemble the roll:* Place the dough on a lightly floured work surface and roll it out until you have a 10 inch by 12 inch rectangle. Spread the walnut mixture over the dough leaving a border about 1 inch wide on all four sides.

6. Carefully lift one of the long sides of the rectangle and roll it up, stopping at the centre of the rectangle. Now begin at the opposite side of the rectangle and roll it until the two rolls meet in the centre.

7. Lift the nut roll onto an oiled baking tray (this is easier if you use two spatulas), and bake for 30–35 minutes, or until pale golden. Cool and serve the nut roll sprinkled with powdered sugar.

Preparation time: 1 hour   Yield: 10 slices
Baking time: 30 -35 minutes

Tahini Cake
Tahinópita

8 ounces dates
1/2 cup tahini
1/2 cup sugar
2 tablespoons honey
2 cups self-rising flour
1 teaspoon cinnamon
5 tablespoons orange juice
1 cup finely chopped walnuts

1. Preheat the oven to 350°F.

2. Pit the dates and cut them into small pieces, put them to soak in 1 cup of hot water.

3. Beat the tahini with the sugar and the honey in a mixing bowl. Add the dates with their water, the flour, cinnamon and a pinch of salt and stir well.

4. Stir in the orange juice and the walnuts, the result will be a thick batter.

5. Spoon the batter into a 9-inch springform pan and bake for 40 minutes.

Preparation time: 30 minutes   Yield: 8–12 servings
Baking time: 40 minutes

Peach Tart
Tárta me Biskóta

Base:
12 ounces Graham crackers
2 tablespoons sugar
1 1/2 teaspoons cinnamon
6 tablespoons margarine, melted

Filling:
1 large (28 ounce) can sliced peaches in syrup
3 tablespoons sugar
1 teaspoon vanilla essence
1/4 cup cornstarch

1. *Prepare the base:* Process the cookies in a food processor until they are finely ground. Place them in a mixing bowl and add the sugar, cinnamon and melted margarine. Mix until they are well combined.

2. Place the cookie mixture in the base of a 9 inch springform pan and press it into an even layer with the back of a fork. Place it in the fridge to cool, about 1 hour.

3. *Prepare the filling:* Drain the peach slices, reserving the syrup. Set the peaches aside.

4. Measure the syrup and add sufficient water to give a total of 2 cups of liquid. Place this in a saucepan and add the sugar, vanilla essence and cornstarch.

5. Heat gently, stirring with a wire whisk, until the mixture simmers and thickens. Cook for another two–three minutes and remove it from the heat. Allow to cool, stirring regularly.

6. *Construct the tart:* Pour the cooled mixture over the base of the tart and arrange the peach slices over the surface.

Refrigerate the tart for at least one hour before serving.

Preparation time: 45 minutes
Refrigeration time: 2 hours

Yield: serves 6

Pumpkin Pie
Kolokythópita

1 small (4 1/2 pounds) pumpkin, or 2 1/2 pounds zucchini
3 tablespoons margarine
6 tablespoons cream of wheat
2 cups shelled walnuts, ground
1/2 cup raisins
1/2 cup sugar
1 pound phyllo dough, defrosted
1/2 cup vegetable oil

1. *If using pumpkin:* Halve the pumpkin, scoop out the seeds. Place each half, cut side down, on your chopping board and slice off the skin. Cut the pumpkin into pieces and grate them (this is easier in a food processor fitted with the grating disk).

2. *If using zucchini:* Rinse, peel and grate them.

3. Place the pumpkin or zucchini in a colander and sprinkle with 2 teaspoons of salt. Let stand for one hour then press well to remove excess moisture.

4. Melt the margarine in a large pot; add the cream of wheat and stir over medium heat for two minutes. Add the pumpkin, walnuts, raisins and sugar and stir well. Remove from the heat.

6. Preheat oven to 350°F.

7. Oil a 13x9x2-inch baking dish and lay half of the phyllo leaves in the base of the dish; brush each leaf with oil as you work. Do not worry about being neat and tidy here: It is better to allow the pastry leaves to lay with some folds and pleats in the dish. This makes a lighter, less compact crust. Simply ensure that you fill the dish evenly.

8. Spread the pumpkin mixture evenly over the phyllo and cover it with the remaining phyllo leaves, using the remaining oil to brush each leaf as you work.

9. Use a sharp knife to score the pie into 12 pieces. Add 1/4 cup of water to any leftover oil and pour this over the pie. Bake for 1 hour.

Preparation time: 45 minutes
Standing time: 1 hour
Baking time: 1 hour

Yield: 12 servings

Raisin Bread
Stafidópsomo

3/4 **cup sugar**
1/2 **cup oil (vegetable or olive oil)**
1/2 **teaspoon baking soda**
3/4 **cup orange juice**
1 **teaspoon grated lemon peel**
1 **teaspoon vanilla essence**
2 **cups all-purpose flour**
1/4 **teaspoon ground clove**
1/2 **teaspoon ground cinnamon**
1 **teaspoon baking powder**
1/2 **teaspoon salt**
1 **cup golden raisins**

1. Preheat the oven to 350°F and grease a medium loaf pan.

2. Beat the sugar with the oil.

3. Dissolve the baking soda in the orange juice, and add this to the sugar mixture with the lemon peel and vanilla essence.

4. Combine the flour, clove, cinnamon, baking powder and salt. Add the liquid ingredients to the flour mixture, stirring well.

5. Rinse and dry the raisins; toss them in 1–2 tablespoons flour and stir them into the batter.

6. Spoon the batter into the loaf pan and bake for 1 hour.

7. Allow the loaf to stand for 10 minutes in the pan. Remove it from the pan carefully and place on a rack to cool completely.

This improves if it is wrapped in aluminum foil and stored in a dry place until the following day.

Preparation time: 30 minutes   Yield: 1 medium loaf
Baking time: 1 hour

Orange Cake
Poudínga Portokaliou

Cake:
1 cup margarine at room temperature
1 1/2 cups sugar
1/4 cup brandy
Finely grated zest of half an orange
1/2 cup orange juice
1/2 cup water
3 cups self-rising flour
1/2 cup raisins
1/2 cup blanched, ground almonds

Syrup:
1 cup sugar
3/4 cup water
2 tablespoons brandy

1. Preheat the oven to 350°F.

2. Beat the margarine and the sugar until light and soft. Gradually beat in the brandy and the grated zest.

3. Add the orange juice to the water. Add one cup of the flour and 1/3 of the orange juice and water to the margarine mixture and stir gently until it is absorbed. Repeat this until all the flour and liquid have been incorporated.

4. Stir in the raisins and almonds and spoon the mixture into a greased 13 x 9-inch rectangular baking pan.

5. Bake for one hour, until golden. Allow the cake to cool.

6. *To make the syrup:* Combine the sugar, water and brandy in a saucepan. Heat and stir until the sugar dissolves then let it boil for 3 minutes. Pierce the cake in a couple dozen places with a skewer or a toothpick and pour the warm, but not hot, syrup over the cake.

Preparation time: 30 minutes   Yield: 12 servings
Baking time: 1 hour

Rolled Baklava
Saraglí

PHYLLO DOUGH can be purchased, frozen, from many supermarkets or from Greek or Middle Eastern food stores. Allow sufficient time for the dough to defrost and do not open it before you are ready to use it. Keep it wrapped in plastic whenever it is not in use, otherwise it will become dry and brittle and impossible to work with.

1 **pound phyllo dough, defrosted**
14 **ounces walnuts, ground**
1 **tablespoon ground cinnamon**
1/2 **pound margarine**

Syrup:
3 1/2 **cups sugar**
3/4 **cup corn syrup**
2 **cups water**

1. Mix the cinnamon with the ground walnuts and divide the mixture equally between two bowls, set one of the bowls aside.

2. Melt 1/4 pound of the margarine.

3. Unwrap the phyllo dough and divide it into two stacks. Re-roll one stack, cover it with plastic wrap and set it aside.

4. Place one sheet of phyllo dough on your work surface and brush it with melted margarine. Stack a second and third sheet over this, brushing each layer with margarine.

5. Sprinkle the third layer with 3–4 tablespoons of the walnut mixture. Continue to add layers of pastry dough (do not brush them with margarine), sprinkling each additional layer with the walnut mixture.

6. When the layers are complete, place a clean knitting needle along one of the short edges and roll the pastry up around it. Slip the needle out of the centre of the roll, place the rolled pastry seam side down, brush it with melted margarine and slice it into 3/4-inch slices.

7. Place the slices, cut side down, on an oiled baking sheet (with sides) and drizzle 2 teaspoons of margarine over each piece.

8. Preheat the oven to 400°F.

9. Melt the remaining margarine and repeat steps 4–7 with the remaining ingredients.

10. Bake the pastries for 7 minutes; reduce the heat to 350°F and bake for a further 7–8 minutes, until they are pale golden.

11. *Prepare the syrup:* Place the sugar, corn syrup and water in a saucepan and bring them to a boil, stirring until the sugar is dissolved. Allow the syrup to simmer at a steady pace for 5 minutes then remove it from the heat and allow it to cool.

12. Cool the pastries on the baking sheet for about 15 minutes. Pour the cooled syrup over the pastries and allow them to stand for 20–30 minutes to soak up the syrup before removing them to a serving platter.

Preparation time: 1 hour   Yield: 24 pieces
Standing time: 30 minutes